Frankly, My Dear

Frankly,

YALE UNIVERSITY PRESS   NEW HAVEN & LONDON

My Dear

Gone with the Wind

Revisited

Molly Haskell

Also by Molly Haskell
From Reverence to Rape: The Treatment of Women in the Movies
Love and Other Infectious Diseases: A Memoir
Holding My Own in No Man's Land: Women and Men and Film and Feminists

Copyright © 2009 by Molly Haskell.
All rights reserved.
This book may not be reproduced, in whole or in part, including illustrations, in any form (beyond that copying permitted by Sections 107 and 108 of the U.S. Copyright Law and except by reviewers for the public press), without written permission from the publishers.

Designed by Sonia Shannon.
Set in Janson by Integrated Publishing Solutions, Grand Rapids, Michigan.
Printed in the United States of America by
R.R. Donnelley, Harrisonburg, Virginia.

Library of Congress Cataloging-in-Publication Data
Haskell, Molly.
Frankly, my dear : Gone with the wind revisited / Molly Haskell.
p. cm. (Icons of America)
Includes bibliographical references and index.
ISBN 978-0-300-11752-3 (cloth : alk. paper)
1. Gone with the wind (Motion picture)   2. Mitchell, Margaret, 1900–1949.
Gone with the wind.   I. Title.
PN1997.G59H37 2009
791.43'72—dc22
2008037296

A catalogue record for this book is available from the British Library.

This paper meets the requirements of ANSI/NISO Z39.48-1992
(Permanence of Paper).

10 9 8 7 6 5 4 3 2

To My Girlfriends
Northern and Southern
And, always,
to Andrew

Contents

Introduction

If ever there was a film that needed no introduction, it would be *Gone with the Wind*. Yet that may be just why it does. Seventy years old and still running strong, thanks to television, DVDs, and revivals that roll around as regularly as national holidays, the movie has acquired both the contempt and the indulgence of familiarity. Its characters have lodged in our unconscious like family members. Its images (the staircase, the green velvet curtain dress) and dialogue ("I don't know nuthin' 'bout birthin' babies") are the stuff of parody and late-night comedy, part of our hearts and funny bones but rarely calling on our more analytical faculties.

David O. Selznick's grand and grandiose three-and-a-half hour production was Hollywood at its most extravagant, the jewel in the crown of a kind of studio moviemaking that would never again be possible . . . or even desirable. It was 1939, war was about to break out, most people were still in the midst of the Depression. Yet in an industry relatively immune to the downturn, a whole galaxy of behind-the-scenes genius craftsmen could conjure up entire worlds on a back lot—a parallel universe where the immortals were more seductive, the colors more ravishing than anything in nature, and everything grimy, unkempt, and discordant was swept under the rug. It's a fitting irony that the example par excellence of this studio-confected world was *Gone with the Wind*, a celebration of caste and class from the New World's most democratic medium, the portrait of a never-never land whose harmony and grace depended on the smoothing out of much that was ugly and uncomfortable.

How something so full of contradiction and dissonance appears so seamless and has proved so enduring is a mystery made possible by our investment in the fantasy, often correcting or "improving" on the book or movie. Viewers and readers misremember a scene or character—for example, forgetting or eliminating Rhett's patrician background. And there are the untold (and told) versions of Scarlett and Rhett getting together in the end.

As with many popular films, especially with stars as charismatic as Vivien Leigh and Clark Gable, emotional appeal and secret fantasy run roughshod over ideology, and something in us resists bringing our two warring sides into daylight scrutiny. Both much beloved and taken for granted, *GWTW* (initials recognizable worldwide) has settled into grooves well worn not only by time but by the way memories fueled by romantic yearnings have formed around it, become indistinguishable not only from our real-life memories but from our very identities.

Of course we want to believe that all things are possible and tomorrow is another day, but at the same time, if we don't want to be stuck forever in Scarlett mode, it might make sense to look again at the movie around her and the part it has played in our lives, personal, political, and social. Investigate it anew for its own intriguing self and for all that has happened, ideologically, politically, cinematically since its opening and, in effect, in its influential wake.

On the downside: as with *Birth of a Nation*, the half-truths of the film both encapsulated and made history: Margaret Mitchell was deeply influenced by D. W. Griffith, and both films' portraits of Reconstruction as an unalloyed horror became the standard view, with the terrors posed by integration more potent than any political countermovement. It awaited later decades and revisionist historians like Eric Foner to set the record straight. *Gone with the Wind*'s portrait of a noble South, martyred to a Lost Cause, gave the region a kind of moral ascendancy that allowed it to hold the rest of the country hostage as the "Dixification" virus spread west of the Mississippi and north of the Mason-Dixon Line. Generations of canny politicians, native sons espousing conservative and racist politics, dominated Washington from Reconstruction up until Civil Rights.

On the other hand, Vivien Leigh's Scarlett, in all her selfishness and intrepidity, is one of the great, iconoclastic figures in movies, a byword for "gumption" and survival, a heroine who grows more astonishing over time. Scarlett's radical refusal of the rules of Southern Christian ladylike behavior, her horribleness and deceitfulness, her cumulative sins and improprieties blaze forth in a strange and ambiguous villainy. Her flaws are never excused but are somehow extenuated by her remarkable courage and resiliency. Never was there a heroine so admirable, so despicable, and above all so beyond the reach of the double standard that traditionally closes in on women in Hollywood films and allows them so little moral and behavioral leeway. She is eerily timely, channeling the spirit of an age, Mitchell's youth-obsessed twenties, that resembles ours to a jarring degree. In Scarlett, the post-suffragette flapper meets the postfeminist power girl, a Madonna derivative, morphing easily into the unbridled capitalist and slave driver (literally) of postwar Atlanta. This is the awesomely shrewd businesswoman who subverts the ethics and threatens the masculinity of the dear white honorable, paternalistic Southern gentleman.

Underneath the nostalgia and high romance (romance, take note, that emanates from the male figures rather than the female), there's something both deeply Southern and deeply American in this wily, sexually repressed, but infinitely resourceful figure: Scarlett embodies the secret masculinization of the outwardly feminine, the uninhibited will to act of every tomboy adolescent, here justified by the rule-bending crisis of war.

It's fascinating to figure out how a film that should never have worked (too many cooks) *did*—in my opinion, largely because of the fire and desperation of three people with strangely overlapping tastes and eccentricities: David Selznick, Margaret Mitchell, and Vivien Leigh.

For those of us who fell under its spell, the range of emotions attached to the film fluctuate over time with the predictable volatility of a love affair and its aftermath, in my own case what we might clinically designate as the Seven Stages of *Gone with the Wind*: Love, Identification, Dependency, Resentment, Embarrassment, Indifference, and then something like Half-Love again, a more grown-up affection informed by a film lover's appreciation of the small miracle by which a mere "woman's film" with a heroine who never quite outgrows adolescence was transfigured into something much larger, something profoundly American, a canvas that contains, if not Walt Whitman's multitudes, at least multiple perspectives.

Frankly, My Dear

ONE

The American Bible

David O. Selznick, Hollywood's self-appointed reader-in-residence, was convinced audiences would sit still for adaptations of famous books, preferably from the nineteenth century and preferably British. The producer had proved it with *Little Women*, *David Copperfield*, and *A Tale of Two Cities*, three certifiable winners, and what was *Gone with the Wind* but a nineteenth-century novel in twentieth-century covers . . . or a twentieth-century novel in nineteenth-century clothing? His other article of faith was fidelity to the source, especially when the work was as widely read and fresh in people's minds as Margaret Mitchell's *Gone with the Wind*. To Sidney Howard, the screenwriter, he recommended making large rather than small cuts, in that "minor changes may give us slight improvements, but there will be five or ten million readers on our heads for them, where, for the most part, they will recognize the obvious necessity of our making drastic cuts." He even urged against changes in construction, because "I have learned to avoid trying to improve on success. One never knows what chemicals have gone to make up something that has appealed to millions of people."

In another memo, Selznick referred to the novel as the American Bible, though with an ulterior motive: he was writing to the censor Will Hays, trying to get "damn" into the punch line at the end of the movie. There's violence and rape, there are curses and improprieties in the Bible, was the implication, so why not in *Gone with the Wind*? And besides, Selznick lectured, "damn" was not a curse but a "vulgarism," so described in *The Oxford English Dictionary*.

It was therefore a fairly big deal when, in a rare deviation from the sacred text, David Selznick decided that *Gone with the Wind*'s ending had to be changed for the movie version. The book's ending was too downbeat, too anticlimactic. After Rhett's departure with the immortal and now officially authorized valedictory, "Frankly, my dear, I don't give a damn," a devastated Scarlett would still decide to return to Tara, to Mammy, to regroup for the possible recapture of Rhett. But Selznick needed to bring Scarlett out of the fog of fear and defeat and give an uplift to the famous concluding line from the book, "Tomorrow is another day." To this end the ghostly voices of her father, Rhett, Ashley would recall to her the magic of Tara, the importance of the land, her one true love. Whereas in the book, Scarlett's thoughts of winning Rhett back are uppermost ("There had never been a man she couldn't get, once she set her mind upon him"), the movie wafts to its end with the softer and more ennobling image of her attachment to Tara.

It's anybody's guess whether the devious charmer we've come to know as Atlanta's most fun-loving shopaholic and shrewd entrepreneur would be content to remain down on the farm, but it's a testimonial to the conviction of this strangely enduring American epic and Vivien Leigh's uncanny performance that we willingly suspend skepticism and accept Scarlett's bond with the land as something fundamental and spiritual, almost redemptive.

Much of the credit for the effectiveness of the denouement goes to the art direction of William Cameron Menzies and the movie's bold, even gothic, use of Technicolor. The spell has been cast by the early scene in which Gerald O'Hara and Scarlett stand under the gnarled bough of a tree, overlooking Tara. The plantation is aglow in a fiery sunset, and the two figures in burnt silhouette suggest both the end and the beginning of the world. The return of that image in the final moments, the visual sweep echoed in Max Steiner's swelling score, completes the emotional sanctification of the land as transcendent value, cemented by the alliance of the daughter with the father, whose Irish blood has by this time marked her character so much more forcefully and balefully than the bluer blood of her Savannah mother.

In a curious way, yet consistent with their different sensibilities, Selznick's ending is more romantic than Margaret Mitchell's, its sense of hope and optimism grounded, literally and figuratively, in something more substantial than Scarlett's wish-fulfillment fantasies. (The inveterate hopefuls among Mitchell fans and the best-selling sequel to the contrary, can anyone over the mental age of fifteen believe that the star-crossed lovers will "get together" one day? Or that they *should?* Even preview audiences, not the most sophisticated crowd and notoriously disposed to feel-good resolutions, but with divine authority where Selznick was concerned, had no objections to the "unhappy" ending.)

The idea of the moral superiority of the land over other forms of acquisition, the legacy of Thomas Jefferson, is one of our most stubbornly enduring myths, persisting despite the continuous and increasing migration to the cities and cherished even among those whose closest acquaintance with a working farm is the occasional drive-by purchase of strawberries or corn at a roadside stand. Or, in the case of Selznick, who made his first trip south for the premiere of the film, viewing gorgeously evocative sketches on a Hollywood storyboard. Land as a lost paradise is but one of the mythic strands whereby the tale of a recalcitrant corner of the country—or, rather, a tiny segment of that corner!—the antebellum, slave-owning renegade South, is alchemized into a national epic of struggle and triumph.

If not exactly the "story that belongs to all of us," as the producer boasted of the 1936 Pulitzer Prize–winning novel he was bringing to the screen, *Gone with the Wind,* in both novel and movie form, can claim to have appealed to the fantasies of a remarkably large number of people. And to have gone on doing so long after its sell-by date. In box office terms, with a domestic gross of $1,329,453,600 adjusted for inflation, it remains the biggest blockbuster of all time, surpassing (after having paved the way for) such runaway hits as *Star Wars, The Sound of Music, E.T.,* and *Titanic.* The only "phenom" to have come close in recent years is not a movie at all but the sleekly murderous and misogynous video game *Grand Theft Auto,* a kind of white man's revenge on Scarlett and all the brainy babes who have threatened to make them obsolescent.

Costing an unprecedented $4,250,000 to produce, *Gone with the Wind* was the first "event" film, and for better and mostly worse, its surprising success changed the way Hollywood thought about movies, whetting its appetite for winner-take-all box-office bonanzas. It was the longest and most expensive film ever made; it went on to earn the highest receipts and win the most Academy Awards. By 1987, in 1987 dollars, Metro-Goldwyn-Mayer theatrical rentals ran to over eight hundred million dollars. In its first run, the movie sold 202 million tickets, a stunning figure considering that the U.S. population was only a little over 130 million at the time. No less dazzling and enduring has been the popularity of the book. If Macmillan editor and scout Harold Latham had "sniffed" a best seller when he read the manuscript, no one at the publishing company was prepared for the extent of its popularity, especially at an astronomical three dollars a copy. It went through multiple printings and continued to sell robustly, thanks no doubt partly to the movie, and to date has sold more than twenty-eight million copies worldwide.

It has inspired sequels and prequels, satires and send-ups. Alexandra Ripley's nearly unreadable *Scarlett*, with the heroine returning to her Irish "roots" and getting rescued from political rioters by an opportunely arriving Rhett, was nevertheless a best seller. Carol Burnett got one of her best skits swathed in the green velvet curtains of Tara's mistress on her way to con money out of Rhett. One look at the curtain rods jutting out like extreme shoulder pads and the audience didn't even need to be told who she was. It has provoked fictional anti–*Gone with the Wind* responses from African Americans, most famously and litigiously *The Wind Done Gone*, by Alice Randall, which as "parody" escaped attempts by the Mitchell estate to block publication. In 1966, an African American writer named Margaret Walker published *Jubilee*, in which a strong mulatto slave named Vyry, a more youthfully attractive, take-charge version of Mammy, tends a depressed and addled mistress. More oblique resistances to the book's generic portrait of passive and contented slaves have come from Alice Walker, Mary Condé, Toni Morrison, and Gloria Naylor.

Gone with the Wind has proved endlessly pliable to reinterpretations, a story to remake or modify according to competing personal mythologies, disturbing—even terrifying—in its power to override reality, ideology, and common sense. The spin-offs and sequels continue to multiply, thanks to the presumed wishes of hordes of people who, like Kathy Bates's murderous fan in *Misery*, will not let Rhett and Scarlett die or go their own ways. And the dollar-minded Mitchell estate is apparently happy to comply with projects as long as they don't sully or snicker at Saint Margaret's version or turn the characters gay.

Rhett Butler's People, Donald McCaig's best-selling prequel of 2007, gives us the "backstory" of Rhett, a revisionist reading of Rhett's plantation childhood as a young master averse to taking up the seigneurial reigns. In this more politically acceptable rendition of Low Country life, the little turncoat-in-the-making prefers to hunt, fish, and pick cotton with the black boys. (Be advised: plot giveaway ahead.) The novel opens with a duel, in which the adult Rhett defends Belle Watling's honor against her white-trash brother's crude aspersions, and ends . . . yes, happily. Amid an extended family and staff that include all extant blacks and whites, Scarlett and Rhett look back with fond humor on all their foolishness, Scarlett appreciates Rhett's enabling hand in her own transformation ("I was a child, Rhett helped me become who I am"), and Scarlett and Belle even become gal pals.

Undeterred by the fate of a musical some years ago that began in Tokyo, stopped off in London, and flamed out in Atlanta, and as a testament to the philosophy that tomorrow is another day, a three-and-a-half-hour musical recently staggered into London's West End and soon met a predictable demise. Rather impressively, the author of the new show's book was a fifty-three-year-old American named Margaret Martin. Once a battered teenage mother who slept on an office floor with her two children, Martin understood Scarlett's struggle with poverty but made rather better use of it, achieving a doctorate in public health and founding a nonprofit agency. Her determination proved equal to writing the book, winning over the Mitchell estate, and securing Trevor Nunn as director but faltered in the face of an artistic impossibility.

Scarlett and Rhett may not be on the same level as such towering archetypes of American literature as Captain Ahab, Daisy Miller, Isabel Archer, Huck Finn, and Hester Prynne or even such cinematic monuments as Charles Foster Kane and John Wayne's Ethan Edwards in *The Searchers*, but they occupy a more personal, familial place in the fantasies of their admirers. They can't be laid to rest because, in ways both touching and frightening, they've become incorporated into the personal lives and dreams of viewers and readers, living on in images mutated by memory and intertwined with desire. A Southern friend decided to read *Rhett Butler's People* to his ninety-year-old bedridden mother. Her favorite book had always been *Gone with the Wind*, and she was ecstatic at the amplification.

"I didn't know all that about Rhett Butler's background, it's just fascinating," she commented to her Northern daughter-in-law who (spoilsport) reminded her that they were not real people but fictional ones—you know, made up. Refusing to believe it, this bright and normally quick-witted matriarch summoned her sons to uphold the biographical veracity of *Gone with the Wind.*

To be fair, it *does* get confusing. In the venerable tradition of the historical novel, Margaret Mitchell throws in a few real names among her fictional characters. Alexander Stephens, the Georgia vice president of the Confederacy, congressman, and governor who inspired a fascinating chapter in Edmund Wilson's *Patriotic Gore,* hovers in the wings. And Scarlett's firstborn (not in the movie) is named after my great-great-grandfather Wade Hampton, the South Carolina general (later governor) whose cavalry Charles Hamilton gallops off to join at the outbreak of war. It is in the general's service that Charles ignominiously dies of measles, leaving Scarlett pregnant with poor, puny Wade Hampton Hamilton.

There's often a curious, very personal logic in the things people remember and misremember about the film. A middle-aged woman insisted to me that Melanie's second child, the one whose miscarriage causes her death, was fathered by Rhett Butler. Beyond whatever interest this wildly eccentric fantasy might have for the woman's psychiatrist, it recognizes the special and profoundly felt mutual respect in the Rhett-Melanie relationship, the exquisite balance between her shyness and his courtliness, that becomes conspiratorially intimate in the scenes where he breaks down and confides in her. Allowing them a moment of mutual gratification, however out of character, is the sort of interactive "intervention" that the book and movie have inspired, in this case to "make amends" to Rhett for the way he has suffered.

With something so embedded, even embalmed, in the public consciousness, the idea of an authorized sequel or a preapproved spin-off is a joke. Whatever the legal statutes and limitations (and Mitchell, the daughter and sister of copyright lawyers, was a shrewd protector of her property), *Gone with the Wind* has long since passed into the public domain—does, indeed, belong to everyone. In 2008, a year of bitter political feuding, Scarlett was invoked by columnists as a Hillary avant la lettre, the only heroine strong, bitchy, and relentless enough to compare with the I'm-no-lady senator's aggressive take-no-prisoners campaign. In this way, *Gone with the Wind*'s touchstones have become American folklore, part of the way we imagine our national self, not just indistinguishable from but overriding real history. Twelve Oaks and Tara are familiar tourist stops in our collective "memory" of the Old South. "I'll think about that tomorrow" and "Tomorrow is another day" have, along with "Frankly, my dear, I don't give a damn," become catchphrases of the American vernacular. Scarlett's seventeen-inch-waist and green velvet curtain dress are the stuff of parody. EBay lists an inexhaustible supply of memorabilia.

Yet no one, not even Selznick, with his inflated claims and over-the-top enthusiasm, could have predicted *Gone with the Wind*'s global reach and longevity, the way both movie and book caught on and grabbed audiences at so many levels and seemed at home in so many eras.

A large part of it was an accident of timing, a coinciding of war and the Depression. Though Mitchell began writing the book in 1926, out of her own generation's postwar spirit of rebellion, creating in Scarlett a Jazz Age heroine transplanted to the Civil War, when the book was finally finished and published in 1936, with the movie following in 1939, it was the Depression that weighed on everyone's minds. According to the cards of the preview audiences, almost all saw the movie as a reflection of their own experience. To these viewers *Gone with the Wind* was both escape and parallel: a story of struggle and survival during a national catastrophe, but at a romantic remove. Scarlett's evolution from seductress to woman of action exerted an enormous pull as a fable for working women, those women and wives who'd had to take over in the absence of men and in a society that otherwise disapproved of women, especially married women, working. It was the woman's angle that Kay Brown, Selznick's canny assistant, responded to; it was she who pushed for purchasing the movie rights and enlisted financier Jock Whitney on her side.

For still others, it was a reminder of a war just past, the loss of lovers, husbands, and brothers in the Great War. And it fell eerily in the shadow of a war to come. Nor were men, despite the story's overpowering appeal to women, excluded from the circle of charm of what became a genuine "crossover" book and movie. Though it had none of the battle scenes that technically constitute a war film (an absence regretted by some reviewers), to most it has seemed as mired in the chaos of war and bloodshed as any frontline drama, no mere home front view of distant goings-on. And if Vivien Leigh was essential to the movie, so was Clark Gable, exerting a tug of iconic virility.

In Nazi-occupied Europe during World War II, Joseph Goebbels considered the portrait of a people struggling for control of their fate so potentially insurrectionary that he banned both the movie and the book. When the film opened after the liberation, the response was ecstatic. Olivia de Havilland described to writer Gavin Lambert its reception in Paris, where the French saw it as a "story about surviving a defeat; physical survival at any price, as you see it in Scarlett; and the kind of spiritual survival represented by Melanie—the endurance of a system of values from a civilization that has been wiped out." Everywhere in Europe the reaction was similar. In Amsterdam and Vienna, says Lambert, "they wept like southerners after the premiere in Atlanta."

In Ethiopia in 1978, *Gone with the Wind* found an enthralled audience among political prisoners jailed by the security forces of Mengistu (Haile Selassie's successor). According to an article in the *American Scholar* by Carol Huang, a contraband copy fell into the hands of a chemistry student, an activist named Nebiy Mekonnen, who began reading the book and translating it into Amharic for his fellow inmates. Mekonnen, whom Huang met in 2004, described being held indefinitely without trial; with fifty men squeezed into a tiny square cell and with no books allowed, the prisoners lived for the daily reading of installments of Margaret Mitchell's story. At first, those who could read English got their turn at the book, but they then gave up the privilege so that Mekonnen could write down the translation on bits of paper from cigarette packs, which were subsequently smuggled out of prison for safekeeping. After his release Mekonnen eventually got the novel published, though ironically with struggles over censorship—the word "slave" was not allowed. But it was the experience in prison that had been a kind of salvation, as men living through an endless night of torture and uncertainty were able to summon courage and hope through Margaret Mitchell's message of survival and the words of Ashley: "In the end what will happen will be what has happened whenever a civilization breaks up. The people who have brains and courage come through and the ones who haven't are winnowed out." Goebbels's fears about the danger posed by the antibodies of resistance released through art were not misplaced.

And then on a whole other level of cultural imprisonment and release was the emerging teenage audience, about to become a social and demographic constituency of its own. Adolescent girls everywhere and for a long time to come would see in Scarlett an emblem of rebellion against tradition and the hypocrisies of their elders. *Gone with the Wind* was a historical romance that transcended the genre with the immediacy of its mix of sex and feminism: an emancipated heroine who transgresses on male turf, a bodice ripper in genteel covers. Girls of ten or twelve or fourteen would stay up all night, reading the book under covers with a flashlight, too young to grasp all its meanings but sensing something utterly fresh—yet safely distanced in time—about the frank self-interest of a sixteen-year-old girl's trashing of social taboos. A friend tells me her first recognizable sexual experience was reading *Gone with the Wind*'s opening page and practically fainting at the description of the Tarleton twins, lounging in their chairs, "their long legs, booted to the knee and thick with saddle muscles, crossed negligently." She had never imagined that boys, or men, could be openly appraised in quite this way.

Northerners were by no means excluded from *Gone with the Wind*'s spell. I know from my New York friends that, like Nancy Drew and Marjorie Morningstar, *Gone with the Wind*, book and movie, was not on any summer reading list but something you discovered on your own and with your friends, a formative experience. Just as we ask, "Where were you when Kennedy was shot?" or "What were you doing on 9/11?" we play "Where were you when you read or saw *Gone with the Wind?*" implying a moment arrested in time, a difference in the before and after. If the Jesuits could boast, "Give me the child until he is seven and I will show you the man," *Gone with the Wind* could make the same claim if it had you by age thirteen or fourteen.

But if Northerners fell in love with the story, in the South it was an obsession. In Richmond, Virginia, in the fifties, when I was a teenager, the effect was momentous, both seductive and incendiary. Reading the book and seeing the movie were to my generation interchangeable rites of passage as inevitable as baptism, the first communion, the first date, the first kiss. It was naughty, but with historical heft and best-seller status; it was dangerous and ought to have been in brown paper cover. It was our first *long* book, before we moved on to Tolstoy and Dostoyevsky. If D. W. Griffith's *Birth of a Nation* was, in part, a recruitment film for the Ku Klux Klan, whose reemergence it inspired, *Gone with the Wind* was a training manual for budding belles, a lesson in the laws of sexual manipulation and flirtation directed toward marriage.

I read and loved the book, but the movie, which I saw after, blazed its images across the page, the two becoming fused in my mind. Where some—a relative few in my experience—disliked the movie for interfering with the Scarlett and Rhett they had vividly imagined, I happily welcomed these bewitching creatures into my pantheon of immortals, little realizing at the time the strength of the impression, how much space they could or would consume, eclipsing and overshadowing "real life" lovers.

And yet I resisted it, too. Both the love and the resistance came from the same place, the experience of being an instinctively self-assertive type in a culture that discouraged female nonconformity. For it had special meaning for girls who grew up like Margaret Mitchell in the deeply conservative South, for whom the Civil War was as yesterday (William Faulkner's definition of the South: the "past . . . not even past"). Like Mitchell, we didn't so much *learn* about the war as emerge from the womb into it. And born as we were into this culture still in thrall to the racism and self-glorification of the Lost Cause, it was our duty to prop up not only Southern pride but the collective male ego that was its cornerstone. As a tomboy determined never to wear lipstick or "play games" of deception, I detested the message peddled by Scarlett, echoing as she did the favorite maxim of our seventh-grade teacher, who daily reminded us that "women rule the world but shouldn't let men know it." Having been schooled in independence by my mother, I found this philosophy, this imperative of deviousness and duplicity, unbearable. I wanted to believe the men I would come to love (if I *did* consent to love) could be dealt with honestly and straightforwardly. Yet my mother was herself a former belle and a consummate lady, and even as I clung to my tomboy prerogatives, I was being drawn along with all my friends into the inescapable vortex of romance, pretty dresses, dances, beaux. From tree-climbing to boyfriend-collecting, the dreaded transition seemed to occur overnight, and with such unholy and unexpected pleasure!

With her own pulls in opposite directions, Margaret Mitchell understood the paradox of a denial rooted deep in the feminine psyche. She had been alternately (in combination and in conflict): tomboy, rebel, flapper, suffragette's daughter, Smith College dropout, debutante, reporter. All this before becoming best-selling author and little lady/housewife of Atlanta. And she knew we were pointed toward marriage like well-trained hunting dogs, yet some of us, like Scarlett and unlike Melanie and Ellen, "found the road to ladyhood hard" and intuited something of the dull and marginalized state of wifehood that went with it.

A movie (or a book) doesn't become a blockbuster by overtaxing its audience with the nuances of history, taking viewers out of their comfort zone with unpleasant truths or partisan issues. *Gone with the Wind*, like most movies, molds history to its own purposes and is in turn molded by our responses. Coming to it at different times in our lives, we get out of it what we are predisposed to "discover," remaking the film according to the zeitgeist. This is particularly true of a movie that covers so much territory, that pushes so many buttons. Unlike, say, *The Wizard of Oz*, released the same year and a perennial though fairly stable favorite, *Gone with the Wind*, with its vast and politically charged canvas, its depiction of the tensions that still underlie our Union, changes over time, some issues receding into the mists of antiquity, others emerging as oddly topical.

As teenagers we respond to its splendor and spectacle, and to one of the most wrenching love stories ever made, and—if only subliminally—to the sexual politics. Even as adults, some remnant of that pure, unskeptical response never leaves us: we hear four notes of Max Steiner's theme song, and we're awash in emotions. There's a primary pull, then a recoil, a secondary period of shame at having been so thoroughly captivated.

The same divisions occur within every group—blacks, critics, feminists. The movie becomes "our" movie by occluding "them": slaves are omnipresent, but the issue of slavery is never raised; there is no indication of its causal relation to the war. Thus is preserved the myth of the South's innocence, that staple of post–Civil War literature and film, about which Arthur Schlesinger remarked, "The North gave to the South in fantasy the victory it had lost in fact." Yet *Gone with the Wind* differs from a long line of Civil War films, particularly popular in the teens and twenties (think *Birth of a Nation*), in which the evil of slavery was blunted out of a twin desire to appease the South and to advance the goal of reunification and nationalism. In the Selznick and Mitchell retelling, Abraham Lincoln is not the honored unifier but the villain of the war, which is caused by his "summoning the troops" and not by Southerners firing on the federal camp of Fort Sumter. Nor is there any hope for reconciliation. In the book's portrait of the war and Reconstruction (toned down in the movie), the Yankees are thoroughgoing scoundrels. Mitchell's novel may be romantic in its love for and abiding loyalty to the South, yet it is skeptical of the Lost Cause mythology. In letters and comments, Mitchell spoke derisively about Thomas Nelson Page, leading practitioner of the moonlight-and-magnolias school of Southern writing, a genre she wanted to avoid at all costs.

This complexity, or contrariness, is what makes the movie so different from, say, *Casablanca* and *The Wizard of Oz*, both of which are iconic but in a more manageable way. There's a consensus about why they're charming . . . or aren't, a common agreement on what's good, bad, silly, and fun. *Gone with the Wind*, on the other hand, with its much wider spectrum, is both different things to different people and different things to the same person at different times in that person's life. Divisions in thinking—the tension between the primitive and the sophisticated, between political advocacy and apolitical enjoyment, between literary (or cinephile) and mass-market taste—have always been there, even constituted part of its pull.

To black activists and most audiences of the politically progressive seventies, it was a cringe-inducing parade of stereotypes. We could hardly look at this movie that seemed to glorify slavery by showing Negroes as supine and docile, only too happy to throw in their lot with their masters. Yet most of us, whites and blacks, have come to appreciate not only many of the performances, particularly Hattie McDaniel's central and all-seeing Mammy, but the stark and groundbreaking drama of Hattie McDaniel herself, daughter of ex-slaves and one-time domestic, winning the Oscar for best supporting actress and gallantly shrugging off her critics.

Ironically reflecting caste and class divisions in the movie, black intellectuals of the thirties deplored both book and movie, but to their chagrin, a great many ordinary blacks lapped them up. And still do. I have it on the authority of a classics professor who taught several years in an ethnically mixed New York City high school that the one book read and loved by all the students in his class was *Gone with the Wind*.

Time has altered our perceptions of race. A younger generation of black women, with the confidence of a few decades of achievement, has been able to tackle the story head-on and use it in complicated and creative ways. Witness the artist Kara Walker's raucous and brilliant panoramas of silhouettes drawn both mockingly and lovingly from the stereotypes of Uncle Remus and *Gone with the Wind*. And at a symposium of black women writers on National Public Radio the participants discussed how they grew up impressed by Scarlett's stubbornness and ambition and, identifying with her, were able to separate out the ugly aspects of slavery from a feeling of kinship with the heroine that transcended race.

The feminist angle, and the movie's profoundly mixed message, came home to me in 1972, when I took part in a panel—one of the first—on the roles of women in film. Gloria Steinem, editor of the newly launched *Ms.* magazine, brought up *Gone with the Wind*, deploring the spectacle of Scarlett being squeezed into her corset to a seventeen-inch waist, that perfect illustration of female bondage, Southern style. I sprang to defend her as a fierce, courageous heroine, going her own way, a survivor, and so on. Both reactions were, in their own way, *right*. But this difference of perspective was also an early augur of the fault lines in feminism or perhaps a necessary split focus: between those predisposed to see and proclaim signs of the victimization of women in a benighted world now progressing toward enlightenment and equality and those inclined to be heartened by the contradictions—the women in the past (both real and fictional) who'd held their own in a chauvinist culture, who'd subverted the norms and gained victories not always apparent through a literal reading of the plot.

For women, the passage that continues to disturb (that is, both excite and perplex) is the famous "rape" scene, when a drunken and frustrated Rhett carries Scarlett up the great winding staircase and has his way with her. Contexts change, perceptions shift, it's one of the things that makes movies such a dynamic medium. What may have gone over the heads and into the hearts of teenagers (as a kind of deserved and sexy punishment) came to seem objectionable in the seventies, when it became vital to wrest the word "rape" from the connotations it had acquired from crime reports, triggering images of male lust and women's complicity. Rape (and the associated wife battery) was a crime of power, not sex (closer to what we think of today as hate crime). But women's so-called rape fantasy, as I wrote in an article for *Ms.*, did not have to be the expression of a masochistic desire for violence, some fearful encounter with an anonymous assailant in a back alley, but rather could be a carefully orchestrated drama of losing control under specific conditions and in well-chosen hands. In other words, it's when Robert Redford (or Clark Gable) won't take "no" for an answer.

In the succeeding years we've had to further modify our understanding of the term, even find different words, according to the way male proprietary aggression is practiced in cultures far removed from our own and involving participants whose feelings we can only guess at. On home ground, our once-straightforward condemnation is complicated by the realization that women themselves possess all sorts of perverse fantasies and appetites that elude the either/or strictures of political correctness.

Scarlett's "rape" scene doesn't end, of course, until the next morning, when we find her curling under the covers, smiling and purring in postcoital bliss. The numbers are legion of Southern ladies of the Victorian sort who married as blushing brides, kept a conviction of virginity through nominal intercourse with their "gentlemen" husbands, even through childbearing, and were then awakened in second marriages by more insistent lovers.

Yes, there are definitely mixed feelings, drawing as the scene does on an episode in Mitchell's own life in which a violent ex-husband returned and invaded her bedroom. But isn't this transformation in feeling and intent the privilege of fiction and the power of movie stars? Mitchell's fictional rape fantasy is a sanitized and eroticized version of a real-life experience that may or may not have included actual rape but in any case wound up in a courtroom.

■

Reviews of both the book and the movie ranged predictably from enthusiastic (the popular press) to denunciatory (the highbrow left) to a more measured middle ground. Donald Adams in the *New York Times Book Review* called Mitchell's work the "best Civil

War novel," while historian Henry Steele Commager in the *New York Herald Tribune* said that despite its melodrama and occasional sentimentally, it "rises triumphantly over this material and becomes, if not a work of art, a dramatic re-creation of life itself." But the book that had beat out Faulkner's *Absalom, Absalom* for the Pulitzer was also excoriated for its politics, for its biased view of Northerners, the war, and Reconstruction, for lacking in personal style . . . for its short-shrifting of history, and especially the causes of the Civil War, and the plight of slaves. For its garrulity and repetition. And . . . for its popularity. As one reviewer pointed out, the novel had more readers than Herbert Hoover had votes in 1932. Malcolm Cowley, whose review for the *New Republic* summed up the view of the literary left, began by serving up quotations from Macmillan's press releases, breathless announcements of successive printings, mounting numbers, and Ripley's-type calculations ("If the copies of *Gone with the Wind* in print were piled on top of each other the stack would be fifty times as high as the Empire State Building") and went on to attack it as "an encyclopedia of the plantation legend" that flattered aristocratic notions. He then itemized the clichés of Southern legend that other writers had dealt in but only "Miss Mitchell" had compiled without leaving anything out:

> The band of faithful retainers, including two that quaintly resemble Aunt Jemima and Old Black Joe; the white-haired massa bathing in mint juleps; the heroine with her

seventeen-inch waist and the high-spirited twins who come courting her in the magnolia-colored moonlight with the darkies singing under the hill—then the War between the States, sir . . . and Sherman's march (now the damnyankees are looting the mansion and one of them threatens to violate its high-bred mistress, but she clutches the rusty trigger of an old horse pistol and it goes off bang in his ugly face)—then the dark days of Reconstruction, the callousness of the Carpetbaggers, the scalawaggishness of the Scalawags, the knightliness of the Ku Klux Klansmen, who frighten Negroes away from the polls, thus making Georgia safe for democracy and virtuous womanhood, and Our Gene Talmadge—it is all here, every last bale of cotton and bushel of moonlight, every last full measure of Southern female devotion working its lilywhite fingers uncomplainingly to the lilywhite bone.

Yet after all this, Cowley concedes not only that the legend has an enduring and fundamental appeal to the emotions but that Miss Mitchell tells it "as if it has never been told before, and [mixes] . . . a good share of realism with the romance." Like so many of the skeptics, he gives with one hand and takes away with the other, so that the admirable "recklessness" with which she attacks her story is that of a blunderer without the writerly experience to be intimidated by comparisons with Dickens or Dostoyevsky. He winds up in a paroxysm of paradox: "I would never, never say that she has written a great novel, but in the midst of triteness and sentimentality her book has a simple-minded courage that suggests the great novelists of the past."

Cowley's wasn't the most dismissive review, but it nettled Margaret Mitchell more than any other. Her reaction, when Stark Young, the Southern novelist and critic, wrote to her about it: "I should be upset and mortified if the left Wingers liked the book. I'd have so much explaining to family and friends if the aesthetes and radicals of literature liked it." The trivializing (and misreading) of the novel particularly centers on the role of women, working their "lilywhite fingers . . . to the lilywhite bone." Lady novelists had become, in the eyes of modernists like Cowley and guardians of the literary canon, something of a plague, with huge numbers of best sellers being "penned" by such as Pearl Buck, Edna Ferber, Vicki Baum, Adela Rogers St. Johns, and Fannie Hurst, usually on themes centering on women—always an inferior subject matter to socially conscious critics of literature and film. The misogyny was characteristic of the time, and the Southern woman in particular was often seen as allied with dangerous, tempting nature; the South itself, social, easy, languid, spoiled, was the female to the North's puritanical energy and masculine drive, a temptation and possibly fatal distraction.

In 1931, while Margaret Mitchell was typing away in secret, five of the best sellers were written by women, and a large number of women's novels were being made into movies in a climate far more hospitable to women than today's Hollywood: the movie of Edna Ferber's *Cimarron* had won an Academy Award, while Pearl Buck's *The Good Earth* had become a best seller. Oscars went to Adela Rogers St. Johns's *A Free Soul* and Vicki Baum's *Grand Hotel*, while Ferber's *Show Boat* was made into a play and (eventually) three movies. It was because of the flowering of Southern women writers like Frances Newman, Ellen Glasgow, and Caroline Miller that Harold Latham from Macmillan had come scouting in Atlanta, a visit that would eventually unearth the manuscript of Mitchell's saga.

The few female reviewers generally bought into this hierarchy of the old-boy network in self-defense. Here is a reviewer (Edith H. Walton) writing for the *New York Times Book Review* on Caroline Gordon's Civil War novel *None Shall Look Back*: "Her style is distinguished—vastly superior, for example, to Margaret Mitchell's; in the clarity and brilliance of her battle scenes she is the equal of MacKinlay Kantor." Gordon gets high marks for unsentimentality and for conceiving her novel "on a heroic scale." Then lip service to canonical values: "Theoretically it is to her credit that she has preferred to dwell on the slow collapse of the Confederacy rather than on the fortunes of private individuals. In practice, however, she sacrifices a good deal by so doing." The review reflects the conventional wisdom that a large canvas is intrinsically superior to a smaller one, that men's actions in war are more important than those of the women who sacrifice and support them, and that, finally, popularity and accessibility are the marks of second-rateness, as if "page turner" weren't the epithet that every author most longs for and fears.

Yes, historical novels by Mitchell's contemporaries are perhaps finer works of literature: but who today reads Gordon, or Young's *So Red the Rose*? Both feature sprawling families, rendered in nuance and detail; their authors know the territory firsthand and are far more penetrating than Mitchell in examining matters of class and caste, but they lack the boldness of conception and the narrative drive, and most of all the set of riveting characters at the front and center that give *Gone with the Wind* its eternally human appeal.

One of the few intellectuals to have deviated from the general tone of condescension was that high priest of mass culture Leslie Fiedler, who championed its pop-cultural appeal as "essentially sado-masochistic." With his peculiar and exuberant sensitivity to perverse subtexts of sex and race, he combined his pet themes, seeing beneath *Gone with the Wind*'s "trappings of High Romance" a "fantasy of interethnic rape as the supreme expression of the violence between the sexes and races."

Fiedler, like D. H. Lawrence, saw the mirroring embrace of blacks and whites as the primary undertow of American culture: the two races were locked together in mutual fantasies of love and hate, rape and murder. Fiedler traces the theme from Mark Twain and Harriet Beecher Stowe through Thomas Dixon and D. W. Griffith to Margaret Mitchell. While acknowledging that the three incidents of rape or intended rape in *Gone with the Wind* don't fit the formula, he nevertheless sees Rhett as a quasi-Negro . . . the "black stranger" from the underworld. This is in line with conjectures, offered by some biographers, of an attraction to mixed-race themes in Mitchell's early writings—a claim disputed by her most recent and thorough biographer, Darden Asbury Pyron. The story in question, "Ropa Carmagin," vanished in the bonfire of Mitchell juvenilia presided over by brother Stephens Mitchell. But reports from those who actually read the sixty-page novella describe a ghost story of postwar decrepitude in a Faulknerian vein, more concerned with spinsterhood than sex, a cautionary tale of "the ancient virgin in a crumbling dwelling."

Fiedler asserts that audiences, while alluding to Scarlett's independence and heroism and the high romance of her vexed relationship with Rhett, are actually (or secretly) most deeply moved by "the nightmare of black insurrection and white violation." Instinctively, I can't agree. But then, as a Southern female for whom romance undoubtedly masked more unacceptable fears and longings, I would be resistant to his formulation, wouldn't I? It was Mitchell's masterstroke to give free play, in the "crossover" figure of Rhett Butler, to dangerous (if not necessarily interracial) desires that the conscious mind would surely reject out of hand. Pyron, who's generally quite aware of the subterranean influences affecting Margaret Mitchell, her skill at disavowing unsavory suggestions, should know that her recoil from sex in general is no argument against the presence of such forbidden urges. And Fiedler is entirely right that only a woman could have written (or gotten away with writing) about a woman being "raped" and liking it.

It's no surprise that the book hasn't found a comfortable resting place in the rambling house of literature, being not so much above criticism as beyond classification, an unholy concatenation of high romance and deftly delivered history, veering in tone and level of accomplishment from the ridiculous to the almost sublime, from reflexive racism to a feelingly accurate attention to the speech and behavior of Negroes, from the pulpier reaches of women's prose to complex historical storytelling that moves at breakneck speed . . . except when it doesn't. The screenwriter Sidney Howard wasn't entirely wrong when he complained, as he skillfully hacked away, that the author repeated everything twice. Nor is it a book that rewards repeated readings. Its strengths and weaknesses are as inseparable as drops of water in a waterfall. For all Scarlett's sizzle and guile and charm, there is something tiresome and claustrophobic about being stuck inside a mind so stubbornly self-reflexive, cloistered in an eternal present, incapable of analysis or retrospection, unable to expand or reconsider.

The movie, concentrating and intensifying the appeal of the characters and eliminating most of the longueurs, came to achieve pride of place in most people's consciousnesses. Yet the same snobbery and distrust of commercial success was characteristic of the cinephiles. The movie was attacked for all the above reasons, plus the gloss and glamorization of the Georgia countryside and

Tara, transformed from Mitchell's rough upcountry farm into a megamansion that bore a remarkable resemblance to Selznick International Pictures, the producer's grandiose columned studio. This edifice, used for Twelve Oaks, was originally Thomas Ince's headquarters, itself modeled on Mount Vernon. The fancy tone was set by Ben Hecht's flourish of a prologue. Hecht had never read the book when David Selznick sent him an SOS to come to Hollywood to work on the script, but his ode might have been a précis of Cowley's review:

> There was a land of Cavaliers and
> Cotton Fields called the Old South . . .
> Here in this pretty world
> Gallantry took its last bow . . .
> Here was the last ever to be seen
> of Knights and their Ladies Fair,
> of Master and of Slave . . .
> Look for it only in books, for it
> is no more than a dream remembered,
> a Civilization gone with the wind.

Mitchell pointed out the incorrectness and absurdity of this inane ditty and Selznick's conception of Tara but knew her efforts on behalf of a more particular truth were no match for Hollywood in full-throttle romanticism, anxious to satisfy the public's vested interest in this myth. She understood that the nostalgia for the "Old South," like all nostalgia, has a life of its own and is all the more powerful when the object of its yearning is more imaginary than real.

In the endless interim between the book's publication in 1936 and the film's opening in 1939, the press had been subjected to a steady barrage of publicity and was sick of the movie before it arrived. The *New York Times*'s Frank S. Nugent seemed to exhale a huge sigh of relief mixed with grudging admiration as he conceded the movie's virtues (the cast, the fidelity of the adaptation) while encapsulating the defects, reaching a conclusion similar to Commager's appraisal of the book: "It is pure narrative, as the novel was, rather than great drama, as the novel was not. . . . You will leave it not with the feeling you have undergone a profound emotional experience, but with the warm and grateful remembrance of an interesting story beautifully told. Is it the greatest motion picture ever made? Probably not, although it is the greatest motion mural we have seen and the most ambitious filmmaking venture in Hollywood's spectacular history."

Great it wasn't, art it wasn't, most critics agreed. Meyer Levin in *Esquire*, expressing the socially conscious approach then favored by movie intellectuals, preferred the first half because it dealt with history and society, while the less politically oriented critics liked the second for that very reason.

Great art or not, it swept the Academy Awards with an unprecedented thirteen nominations (although the New York Film Critics Circle, having fought over *Gone with the Wind, Mr. Smith Goes to Washington*, and *Wuthering Heights*, finally settled on the last as Best Picture). It won Best Picture, Best Director, Best Actress, Best Supporting Actress, Best Screenplay (Sidney Howard, posthumously), Best Art Interior Direction (Lyle Wheeler), Best Film Editing, Best Color Cinematography, a Special Award for William Cameron Menzies, and the Irving J. Thalberg Memorial Award for David Selznick.

Gone with the Wind's Oscar landslide only confirmed its status as that quintessence of middlebrow, a "prestige" film, perfect but impersonal. Indeed, from any aesthetic criteria, it was not one of the all-time great films, not even the best film of 1939, a banner year that produced an embarrassment of riches, including but not restricted to: John Ford's *Stagecoach* and *Young Mr. Lincoln*; Ernst Lubitsch's *Ninotchka*; Leo McCarey's *Love Affair*; Frank Capra's *Mr. Smith Goes to Washington*; Howard Hawks's *Only Angels Have Wings*; George Stevens's *Gunga Din*; George Cukor's *The Women*; Raoul Walsh's *The Roaring Twenties*; Victor Fleming's *The Wizard of Oz*; William Wyler's *Wuthering Heights*; Cecil B. DeMille's *Union Pacific*; Lewis Milestone's *Of Mice and Men*; John M. Stahl's *When Tomorrow Comes*; Mitchell Leisen's *Midnight*; Edmund Goulding's *Dark Victory* and *The Old Maid*; George Marshall's *Destry Rides Again*; Zoltan Korda's *Four Feathers*; Sam Wood's *Goodbye, Mr. Chips*; and Gregory Ratoff's *Intermezzo*.

A little over three decades later, the seventies' spirit of multicultural radicalism that led to a recoil from *Gone with the Wind*'s treatment of blacks also brought a dethroning of high culture in favor of popular culture and a revaluation of American cinema from an auteurist standpoint. This aesthetic point of view recognized how powerfully and significantly directors shaped movies such as those cited above. And in fact, the genius of the system notwithstanding, the movies that have prevailed by any discriminating consensus are those where the genius was in the head of one man rather than diffused throughout a team, bearing the stamp of Fordian or Hawksian or, later, Wellesian individuality. By this generally workable criterion the weakest John Ford film would be superior to the best of Victor Fleming, and *Gone with the Wind*, which had lost an auteur for a journeyman (yea, Cukor; boo, Fleming) was a product of too many different sensibilities. There were actually five directors if you count Sam Wood filling in and two second-unit men brought in after Victor Fleming's collapse from exhaustion; fifteen screenwriters (including F. Scott Fitzgerald and Ben Hecht, though only Sidney Howard received official credit); two art directors; various official and unofficial consultants; and through it all, a manic Selznick popping bennies, up all night, micromanaging and multitasking, sabotaging his own project with endless interference.

It's not by any stretch a personal masterwork like *Citizen Kane*, *The Magnificent Ambersons*, *The Searchers*, and even lesser gems of style and substance. It was put together piece by piece, what one critic called "the supreme custom-built movie," yet there were so many great craftsmen involved in the making that it becomes a strange amalgam of greatness, with even the competing (and complementary) talents of Cukor and Fleming working in its favor.

According to the stern moral axiom that a film can't be both great and popular, our affection for it is almost a mark in its disfavor. It's too prominent on the cultural map to be identified with the furtive byways of the "guilty pleasure." It's shown often on television, it has steady DVD sales, and there have been endless revivals and reruns, both on anniversaries and on years in between. After a big theatrical revival in the watershed year of 1967, when *Bonnie and Clyde* and *The Graduate* went toe to toe for the Oscar with old-fashioned yarns like *Dr. Dolittle* and *Guess Who's Coming to Dinner* and *In the Heat of the Night* (as chronicled in Mark Harris's book *Pictures at a Revolution*), *Gone with the Wind* went on to garner thirty million dollars in re-release.

Neither sufficiently ("exhilaratingly") pulpy nor obliquely masterful, it wouldn't be caught dead in a film class. Yet we seem to acknowledge that there is something not-quite-grown-up-rational in our sneaking fondness for the movie.

The critic Andrew Sarris, from whose hyper-auteurist *American Cinema* index the 1939 list is drawn, puts *Gone with the Wind* at number sixteen (ahead of Victor Fleming's other film of that year, *The Wizard of Oz*), yet I suspect he would have traded them all in for Vivien Leigh's green eyes, a revelation to which only the newly developed (and masterfully adapted) Technicolor process could do justice.

34

It's easy to poke fun at the literary, and sometimes pseudoliterary, ambitions of Selznick, yet he could have lost his reputation as well as his shirt, could have been a laughingstock (and he actually did end up losing a great deal because of his eventual need to sell the film rights to MGM). There were many good reasons (mostly financial) that so few studios were eager to bid on the book, but there was one overwhelming argument in its favor: the generalized nature of the story, the very lack of historical detail with which critics reproached it, allowed it to speak of timeless love and loss, of family and romance, of a titanic struggle against national catastrophe that reverberated with all the struggles, past and to come, in a young nation's history.

Nor is the reference to the Bible merely opportunistic. Margaret Mitchell, like everyone in her generation, was steeped in the holy book. There are biblical echoes (the flight out of Egypt?) when Scarlett, Prissy, Melanie, and Rhett with Melanie's baby surge down the stairs and into the carriage, evacuating Atlanta against a "pillar of fire." And just as the book had none of the archaic, self-conscious, research-heavy feel of the historical novel, so the movie had little of the fussiness and strain of the costume drama. As few writers have done, Mitchell makes the past present, and miraculously, so does David Selznick's adaptation. Thanks to the way Selznick, Vivien Leigh, and Margaret Mitchell, the three driving forces of the movie, poured themselves into it, that historical "costume" story never feels remotely dated. In *Gone with the Wind*, Mitchell's only book, every crisis and trauma of her life is transmuted into narrative; Selznick seized the reins and threw himself into the making of the movie like a man possessed; and Leigh, whose casting was less accidental than legend has it, invested Scarlett with something beyond beauty, something altogether uncanny—a demonic energy, a feverishness that would later tip over into illness and pathology.

During his stint as a movie reviewer, Graham Greene tried, like the best early critics, to understand and describe the new medium on its own terms. "We have to accept its popularity as a virtue," he wrote, "not turn away from it as a vice." Selznick, trying to combine art and commerce, intuitively reached for what Greene defined as a "popular response," "not the sum of private excitements, but mass feeling, mass excitement." Greene might not have admitted *Gone with the Wind* to his populist pantheon—most intellectual champions of pop culture have stringent snobberies of their own. They'll instinctively embrace slapstick comedy, for example, and scorn melodrama, just as women will generally choose a Cary Grant picture over one featuring the Marx Brothers. But *Gone with the Wind* would seem to satisfy, as few movies had, the sense, in Greene's words, "that the picture has been made by its spectators and not merely shown to them, that it has sprung as much as their sports from their level."

In the seventy years since its appearance, there has been nothing like it. There have been war films, films about American presidents (though few, and most about Lincoln), and films about love and loss, but none have managed *Gone with the Wind*'s unique blend of panoramic vision and intense family drama, its portrait of a land riven by war—the deadliest war ever fought on American soil—as seen and experienced by the families who lived, fought, and suffered that war. For whereas most Northerners of "good" families bought their way out of battle through mercenaries and foreign draftees, Southerners across the board— farmers, yeomen, and aristocrats—fought and died in huge, almost unthinkable numbers.

Hence, the Civil War is indeed "our" American war, the one that determined whether we would manage to become a nation, however divided, or a coalition of independently run (and therefore minor) fiefdoms with their own laws and treaties with one another and with Europe. There were more American deaths than in any other war, and it was more wrenching in terms of loyalties, brother against brother, friend against friend. We are, in *Gone with the Wind*, still wrestling with our destiny as a country and with the ambiguities (who won and in what sense) that came out of the war.

Trading in a false nostalgia in the smoothing out of history is, admittedly, the stock-in-trade of best-sellerdom and mass-market Hollywood, the trick of offering "something for everyone." When we deplore such pandering, it is generally from the point of view of a more sophisticated, discerning "we," as opposed to those supine, pap-swallowing audiences to whom we feel superior. Yet the biases of cultural snobbery are often no less reflexive, as we prefer to overlook or ignore disconcerting and contradictory aspects of popular culture that don't support our prejudices and agendas.

If Selznick's movie pandered to a messy democracy's *nostalgie de l'élite*, a yearning for aristocratic Anglo forebears, however factitious, it also challenged the Plantation myth, with an upstart antiaristocratic hoyden tilting at sacred cows and shibboleths. For all her Southern belle qualities, Scarlett possessed precisely those "Yankee" virtues—ambition, greed, industry, and materialism—associated with the New South and despised by Lost Cause romanticists. For her contrariness alone, the movie that surrounds and forgives her warrants a fresh look at the many-layered ambiguities that have caused perspectives to shift and interpretations to change over time.

TWO

Boldness and Desperation

Margaret Mitchell, accident prone, with a sprained ankle that laid her up for months, begins *Gone with the Wind* in 1926. Depressed, she starts with the ending, pours her whole life into the story, hammers away for ten years, squirreling sheaves of barely readable manuscript into manila envelopes, correcting and revising, torn between panic at the thought of publishing—lawsuits, critical scorn, self-exposure—and an equally desperate need to justify her existence as a writer. David Selznick, risking his reputation and career, takes on a project that most of Hollywood reckoned as sheer folly, coasting on a continual high from pill-popping, all-night gambling, and pure chutzpah, his manic perfectionism driving everyone crazy. Vivien Leigh, feverish with as-yet undiagnosed mental and medical problems, longing for

Laurence Olivier, works harder than anyone, giving more to the film, Olivia de Havilland said, "than it ever gave back to her."

Something fierce, something beyond normal ambition united these three, who were so crucial to the success of *Gone with the Wind*; something headlong and hurtling in the intensity of their work; something uncanny and complementary in their contradictions, their ambivalences, the ghosts and demons that drove them separately and together.

Was it "gumption," Margaret Mitchell's favorite word to describe the Darwinian divide between those who made it and those who fell by the wayside? If anyone passed the gumption test for survival it would be Peggy (the nickname she later gave herself) Mitchell, David Selznick, and Vivien Leigh. But the term, like Margaret Mitchell's pose of homespun earthiness, is a little too modest, connoting good old common sense, while what was going on here was way beyond common sense. Something along the lines of what Selznick referred to as desperation. Where did the intensity come from?

First, Selznick and Leigh, and then, with a chapter to herself, Margaret Mitchell. On the producer's part, coupled with and firing the ambition of a second-generation would-be mogul was a burning need to avenge what he saw as the betrayal and humiliation of his father. An immigrant from Russia who first made a success in jewelry on the East Coast, Lewis J. Selznick had been a pioneer of the Louis B. Mayer and Darryl F. Zanuck era. He had gone, according to the biographer David Thomson, "from being a scrambling huckster to one of the most paper-rich men in America," with the Selznick Pictures Corporation organized to contain a whole range of movie interests and projects. But in one of those rounds of cutthroat competition and realignments, and when he could no longer get the A-list stars, he'd gone under. The bankruptcy arose largely through fiscal malfeasance and mismanagement, but the sons blamed the studios for their father's ruination, turning the disaster into a legend of victimization that drove their careers. Charming, creative David and ruthless flesh-peddler Myron would become the good cop–bad cop heroes of their own revenge melodrama: as Hollywood's toughest agent, Myron would stick it to the moguls for enormous sums on behalf of his clients, and wunderkind David would better them at their own game.

The brothers had grown up in the movie business. David started as a story analyst in his mid-teens and was running the publicity department and publishing a weekly newsletter, "The Brain Exchange," for Selznick Pictures by the age of eighteen. Far from advising frugality, the father made a creed of profligacy and risk, insisting that his sons take chances, to the point of giving them huge allowances (Myron, at twenty, was receiving a thousand dollars a week and David, four years younger, $750!). "Always be broke!" he repeatedly told them, an injunction which he only too haplessly fulfilled.

Once David embarked as a producer, bouncing from studio to studio, his gambles paid off handsomely. A unique combination of artistic aspiration and show-business savvy and now, in 1936, the head of his own production company, Selznick International Pictures, he had blazed a trail that was both successful in Hollywood terms and more literate, particularly attuned to the tastes of book-reading females. Girls and young women used to light up with anticipation when they saw the familiar white columns and veranda of the Selznick logo, catnip to that era's version of a "chick-flick" audience that Selznick instinctively and intelligently sought. But underneath that huge ambition and comparative refinement lay a thirst for revenge as powerful as Scarlett's. ("As God is my witness . . . .")

Margaret Mitchell, professing a lack of enthusiasm for the project, expressed the general view when she said it could never be made into a movie. Readers who numbered in the millions would resent any abridgment, and for Hollywood purposes, it was too long, had too many characters, was too expensive. . . . The arguments against it were all but overwhelming, and it wasn't just the length and budget. Costume pictures were out of favor, the Great War had killed the market for war films, and Civil War movies in particular had become box-office poison after the recent failure of *So Red the Rose*. Stark Young's best-selling novel about the Natchez aristocracy was far closer in spirit to Ben Hecht's elegy to the planters and their doomed way of life. There were ironies and complexities that didn't make it into King Vidor's 1935 film, an odd mixture of the absurd and the

stirring. Nothing in *Gone with the Wind*'s portrait of loyal Negroes matches the risible spectacle of slaves cheering when their
master (Randolph Scott) goes off to fight their emancipators.
Generally, though, Vidor's blacks are more sullen and trouble-
some. At one point, they stage a mini-uprising that only Margaret Sullavan's honey-toned belle can quell.

Meanwhile, sneak galleys of the soon-to-be best seller were
smuggled into some of the studios, but Macmillan's asking price
was an exorbitant hundred thousand dollars, and there were few
nibbles even after Annie Laurie Williams, Macmillan's shrewd
subsidiary rights negotiator, came down to sixty-five thousand.

Viewed retroactively, there are more "what-ifs" and "might
have beens" in the making of *Gone with the Wind* than among the
folks of Margaret Mitchell's postbellum Atlanta, who (to Scarlett's bored chagrin) insist on refighting the war at every opportunity, discussing the hypotheses and near-misses that might
have led to Southern victory: "If Jeff Davis had commandeered
all the cotton and gotten it to England before the blockade tight-
ened—"; "If Longstreet had obeyed orders at Gettysburg—"; "If
Jeb Stuart . . ."; "If Vicksburg hadn't fallen—"; "If we could have
held on another year . . . ." And always: "If they hadn't replaced
Johnston with Hood" or "If they'd put Hood in command at
Dalton instead of Johnston"—not to mention the "if" expressed
by the feckless young war veterans Tommy Wellburn and Rene
Picard, forced to put their noses to the grindstone by their new

in-laws, the fearsome Mrs. Elsing and Mrs. Merriwether, "If we'd had our mothers-in-law in the ranks, we'd have beat the Yankees in a week."

The "ifs" of antebellum Hollywood whereby David Selznick might never have gotten the chance to beat the bank or destroy his career are legion. If Kay Brown, Selznick's assistant, hadn't fallen so hard for the book in galleys, and if she hadn't enlisted financier Jock Whitney's support early on. If MGM chairman Nick Schenck hadn't been in the bathtub with a cold when an enthusiastic William Fadiman, sent by L. B. Mayer, arrived at Schenck's Long Island mansion with a synopsis. ("Tell me the story," the bleary-headed executive is reported to have said, in the account by Scott Eyman, and after Fadiman got through: "It's about what . . . a war? Who needs war? Everybody dies." "Well," Fadiman said, "Some do." "Everybody dies. It's sad. You tell Louis, 'No.'")

If either Katharine Hepburn or Bette Davis had gotten the part—though of the two, only Hepburn campaigned for it; Davis fans and surrogates campaigned for her while she fought Jack Warner in a London court. RKO actually put in a bid of fifty-five thousand dollars on Hepburn's behalf, but only after Selznick's fifty-thousand-dollar offer had been accepted.

If instead of being a woman of her word, Margaret Mitchell had reneged on her initial acceptance of Selznick's offer and taken the higher bid from RKO; if the casting of the principals had been otherwise; if Selznick hadn't promised the reluctant

Leslie Howard he could direct his own picture; and the biggest if of all: if MGM had refused to loan out Clark Gable, and if Gable (who disliked Selznick and didn't want to play the role) hadn't desperately wanted to marry Carole Lombard. It wasn't that he had free will; indeed, he was being bartered over, in David Thomson's words, like a "prize bull." As a contract player, he had to do what Metro wanted him to do, but he was so unhappy and unwilling, they sweetened the package with a bonus offer of fifty thousand dollars—the sum he needed to get a divorce from Ria Langham and marry Lombard (who in turn assisted the cause by pressing him to accept the role and take his career more seriously).

The smart money said that *Gone with the Wind* was a film no independent studio could make; Selznick maintained it was a film that *only* an independent company could make. His feeling for the business, combined with a sense of what he wanted to do, had stood him in good stead as he jumped from studio to studio, first Paramount, then RKO, then Metro-Goldwyn-Mayer. At RKO, his feeling for lavishly produced women's stories with strong heroines made his collaboration with George Cukor a natural. Fighting the money men in New York all the way, the two had made *A Bill of Divorcement, What Price Hollywood?* and *Little Women.* The joke, after David went to MGM, the company run by the father of his wife, Irene Mayer Selznick, was "the son-in-law also rises," but the young man was rising plenty fast without L.B.'s help. It wasn't nepotism that brought such phenomenal personal successes as *Dinner at Eight* and, later, *David*

Copperfield. An instant rival, admirer, and friendly colleague of golden boy Irving J. Thalberg, Selznick was an equally shrewd judge of talent, discovering (with Kay Brown's tip) Ingrid Bergman and green-lighting a screen test for Fred Astaire (whom most people saw as an odd duck, too old, with big ears).

Chafing at his inability to push through his pet projects, Selznick had left Metro and the supervision of Mayer to form an independent production company, and now he was back negotiating a tough deal with his father-in-law to get Gable. He had hoped he could make the film for one and a half million without help from Mayer. Warner's proposal of Bette Davis and Errol Flynn was far sweeter financially, and Flynn was one of the less implausible candidates, but America had spoken: Selznick had to have Gable. As it was, Selznick, given no quarter by L.B., had to sign a near-usurious deal with MGM whereby Mayer would get 50 percent of the film's profits and distribution rights (something the much smaller Selznick International couldn't handle), all to get Gable.

Everything that should have sunk the film somehow worked in its favor. All the publicity shenanigans that irritated the finer-grained critics—the hype, the delays, the noisy two-year search for Scarlett (it was also the first case of overhype, to such an extent that even those who hadn't thought Selznick crazy to take it on now predicted that the backlash would do him and the film in)—were a bonanza to the fans. Thanks to David's courtship methods, the public was in on the process from beginning to end to an unusual degree even at that time of heightened studio sensitivity to public opinion.

This was a time of maximum censorship under the stiff rules of the Hays Office, created by the movie industry in the early thirties in response to public and press outrage over Hollywood scandals and pressure from the Catholic Legion of Decency. The Production Code's enforcers, headed by Joseph I. Breen at the Hays Office, read and passed on every script and, anticipating the furor of state and local censorship boards, demanded the elimination of all forms of impropriety. This included profanity, excessive violence, crime without retribution, and most of all any whiff of sex, even the merest suggestion or innuendo. (Rhett Butler's "I want you, Scarlett" raised red flags, as did the line "You should be kissed—and often—and by someone who knows how.") No adultery unless punished by ostracism or an illegitimate child. Women weren't prostitutes but dance-hall girls, party girls, or simply women who smiled at too many men. Married couples slept in twin beds, and if a scene called for a character to be *on* a bed, one foot had to rest firmly on the floor. The list of taboos, laughable today, kept movies safe from contamination until well into the fifties, when the forces of counterculture and sexual liberation overwhelmed the dam. Jokes about Doris Day's prolonged filters-and-Vaseline-protected virginity exposed the prurience of the Hays Code and led to a freeing up of the screen. The counterculture, in rock concerts and films about rock concerts, heralded a new era, and directors and movies more in tune with the new zeitgeist showed Hollywood there was money to be made in anti-Hollywood movies. Women's liberation meant that women's sexuality could be treated more openly on the screen, though whether that proved any great boon to women is another question. Writers and directors in the thirties and forties movies were forced to find ingenious ways of keeping sex front and center in the picture, but obliquely, symbolically. Nor did audiences rise in protest over the repressiveness of the screen and the squeamishness of the movies' moral arbiters. If the Hays Office (aided and abetted by its religious adjunct, the Legion of Decency) was the guardian of a puritanical moral standard, it was one with which the public was in full agreement.

There were polls and there were numbers, but there were also angry letters of protest from individuals or tiny "activist" groups that could make studio executives quail. Any audience member with a beef and a letterhead could vent and get attention. There was great outcry and epistolary hand-wringing over moral degeneration and the celebration of violence and "criminal tendencies" (those very tendencies that would be de rigueur in movies pandering to a youth audience half a century later). A hand-scrawled letter from a Mrs. N of the Milwaukee County Better Films Council found in the Warner Bros. archives complains of *High Sierra*'s "questionable social value" and objects to the sympathetic nature of the criminal. A public relations executive replies at great and courteous length, first with the old Aristotelian cathartic effect argument ("young minds" with an "incipient criminal tendency" will have their impulses reduced through release) and then, even more ingenious, with the assertion that if audiences can identify with the criminal, "they will be more likely to be on their guard, preventing their own bad instincts from gaining the ascendancy."

One detects a lip-smacking tone of disapproval in the memos from Joseph Breen at the Hays Office as he flags particular scenes to Val Lewton, Selznick's intermediary in this affair:

> The business of Scarlett pressing her body against Ashley (a married man) and his reaction of "drawing her tighter and tighter" toward him, should be entirely eliminated.

> The business of Scarlett running her hands over her neck and breasts, and the slight curves of her body, should not be actually shown. It might be acceptable to merely suggest the action, keeping away, of course, from the breasts.

As for Scarlett's visit to the imprisoned Rhett to win money out of him for Tara's taxes, anything that suggests she "offers him her body" cannot be approved. Belle Watling's "establishment" (their quotes) is "overemphasized," and as a prostitute she is made to appear too "sympathetic in contrast to the decent women of your story." Breen suggests that the brothel be changed to a "drinking parlor" or even a "gambling house," and let's not have any "luxurious couch" or Rhett lying around in a dressing gown. Rhett's line about mixing business with pleasure "should be entirely eliminated. Such a line is certain to give enormous offense to women patrons everywhere." The British censors are apparently no less stringent; they won't permit "a couple, even a married couple, occupying the same bed," and are even more excitable over any whiff of even simulated harm to animals. "The business of the horse stumbling" should be deleted, along with any "spectacular" falls from horses. (What the Brits did with little Bonnie's fatal tumble is anyone's guess.)

If producers then and now were in the business of pleasing audiences, the studios then had a wider target: everyone. None of the niche marketing of today. And Selznick was in a class by himself in the special, almost mystical bond he felt he enjoyed with his viewers. The casting search was one he conducted not only in public but with the public, whose opinions and temperature he gauged through polls, letters, newspaper stories, and fan magazines with the assiduity of a private-duty nurse. He'd already done a highly publicized talent search for the child actor who would play David Copperfield, which culminated, alas, in Freddie Bartholomew, whose Anglo-sissy persona (*Little Lord Fauntleroy*) came to dominate little boy roles and made him the highest-paid child actor after Shirley Temple. The Scarlett search offered juicier opportunities: famous casting-couch skirmishes with various aspiring Southern belles. But these flirtations were only one-on-one, conducted, according to the ever-acerbic Evelyn Keyes, who became Suellen, "in a rather obligatory fashion."

This was in stark opposition to the high-intensity courtship dance in which Selznick and his public took turns leading and deferring to each other.

A significant aspect of Selznick's partnership with his public—and this to a heightened degree in the making of *Gone with the Wind*—was his self-appointed role as keeper of the literary faith. Quaint even for the late thirties, when few people were making adaptations of the classics, Selznick was famous for carrying around a dog-eared copy of *Great Expectations*, his favorite childhood book, and *A Tale of Two Cities*, the one, read in adolescence, that influenced his taste for doomed love or, as biographer Ron Haver expressed it, for "thwarted romance and unhappy endings." He would regale listeners with the story of how his father had read all of Dickens to him as a boy, an idea at which the sardonic Joe Mankiewicz scoffed. According to David Thomson in *Showman: The Life of David O. Selznick*, Mankiewicz said of Selznick père, "The old man was barely literate," and stated that David's passion for literature was in the service of something he enjoyed even more, beginning with an "f." Mankiewicz noted that anyone in Hollywood could pose as an expert on the classics simply by reading the Great Books synopses that circulated from studio to studio. But even if Selznick's in-depth reading was just a seduction ploy, it was one on a large scale, and an intrinsic part of his self-image, the literary man in Hollywood, the rigorous adapter of classical works, keeping faith with his audience by keeping faith—in this case—with the "American Bible." We can laugh at his messianic fervor, but this same quality made him fight as no one else would have to retain the seditious and improper charms of *Gone with the Wind*, including the famous battle over the word "damn." He also knew when to let well enough alone. When Sidney Howard pointed out that Mitchell repeated herself, he concurred: "An outstanding case of this is the repetition of what you might describe as 'nights of love.' Certainly, I think one scene of husbandly rape is enough. How the hell we can even use one is going to be a problem."

This was all rather ironic in light of Mitchell's own attitude, found in her letters, that she was attempting to write against the grain of "Jazz Age fiction." She was exasperated, she wrote, at "finding 'son of a bitch' on the first page of every novel. . . . I don't mean to sound prissy because it wasn't that I was shocked but I just got good and tired of it. So I thought I'd try to write a book that didn't use that phrase a single time . . . a book in which no one was seduced and there wouldn't be a single sadist or degenerate. . . . Of course I knew it would never sell but I didn't intend to sell it. I was just writing to keep from worrying about never walking again."

So sick was she of sordid Jazz Age novels, with people jumping in and out of beds, so determined to write a novel with none of these unsavory elements, that she wrote a book that, as she told people later, her own mother wouldn't have let her read until she was eighteen. In any case, by Hollywood standards, it was about as racy as you could (or couldn't) get, with the movie ultimately breaching more sexual prohibitions than any major film of its time—all with the implicit sanction of audiences who would have deplored an actual rape scene, or even the use of the word, but were thrilled when Rhett "punishes" Scarlett for her spiritual infidelity by not taking "no" for an answer.

Initially, Selznick's courtship of his audience focused on the South. He wanted their approval, their permission, so he floated Southern actresses' names and even sent minions to interview possible Scarletts. As part of his natural wish to do well by the book and its constituency and to keep the movie "correct," he pleaded with Margaret Mitchell to come on board, as screenwriter, as adviser, as a presence in Hollywood at whatever level of involvement she might accept. Letters flew back and forth, his usual powers of persuasion unavailing. She was his equal both in forcefulness of personality and in epistolary eloquence and prolixity. Indeed, one of the things they had in common was a compulsive need to scribble letters (or in his case, memos), a logorrhea that seemed to come from similar motives and drives. Both had frustrations as "creative" writers—she would never write another novel, he couldn't leave screenwriters alone but was constantly having his contributions shot down. He had a sufficient sense of his own importance, she of the world's curiosity on her behalf, to want to leave a record for posterity, albeit one of their own designing. And both were simply—and complicatedly—

founts of nonstop verbal exuberance, firing off reams of prose in a hyper-self-aware outpouring of charm and persuasion, prevarication and self-justification.

Repeatedly and in no uncertain terms, she declined his entreaties, wishing to have nothing to do with the movie and any embarrassments it might cause her among the good folks of Atlanta. She wouldn't come to Hollywood but graciously offered to introduce "the Selznickers" to all and sundry. This was her umbrella term for the Hollywood interlopers, Selznick's staff and crew, and included Cukor the director, Walter Plunkett the costume designer, and Selznick himself (who never went). She would show them around Atlanta and its environs, introduce them to the appropriate people, but wouldn't budge or comment on the proceedings. Mitchell had passionate reasons for wanting to keep a low profile and nurtured her own little thirst for revenge.

She had an uneasy relationship with Atlanta society, and the two had collided at a debutante ball. As a freshman at Smith, she'd returned (with some relief; she hated college) to Atlanta when her mother died of the typhoid, and she began taking care of her father and brother and "making a place for herself." As a debutante she was finding a popularity that had hitherto eluded her, but at a ball one evening, the devil in her went too far. She and a young escort, after practicing for days, went through a Valentino-esque series of twirls, embraces, and moves involving hot kisses and mock brutality. The dowager chaperones were horrified, averred that the dance was "too strenuous" (lovely euphemism) for a debutante ball. The incident, covered in the newspaper's social column, created such a scandal that it led indirectly to her being dropped as a candidate for the Junior League. She nursed a grudge. Although she came to embrace wifely domesticity with an almost perverse traditionalism, her fury at the hypocrisies and snobberies of social arbiters like the gorgon Mrs. Merriwether remained steadfast, and when the Junior League threw a party for the *Gone with the Wind* cast at the time of the premiere, she refused to attend.

She'd always resented the power of the biddies and dowagers, the hypocrisies of their gossipy judgments on the younger generation; and now through Scarlett, she could thumb her nose at them. At the same time, she was an Atlanta girl born and bred, loved the city and most of the people in it, and by this time had made her peace with it and had no intention of ever leaving. One of the reasons she dragged her feet on the writing of the book was her fear of wounding sensitivities and, worse, of provoking a libel suit.

There was no way she was going to associate herself with some Hollywood extravaganza that might, with its vulgarizations and simplifications, put her in hot water with the genteel locals. At the same time, she not only wished the film well, she was avid to stay abreast of the proceedings, and she wanted it to be a work she would not be embarrassed by. To this end, she put forward the names of two friends and experts whom Selznick promptly hired: Walter Kurtz, Atlanta's premier Civil War historian and in particular an expert on architecture, and Susan Myrick, a tough-lady journalist and friend who would advise on accents and etiquette. Myrick was a reporter for the *Macon Telegraph*, one of those old-fashioned breed of newspaper "guys" who did everything from book reviews and cooking to covering local stories, particularly those about race.

In the letter of recommendation to Kay Brown, Peggy Mitchell declines once again to come to Hollywood in order to "pass on the authenticity and rightness of this and that, the accents of the white actors, the dialect of the colored ones, the minor matters of dress and deportment, the small touches of color," but enthuses over Susan, a young woman from a good Confederate family fallen on hard times. She is "poor as Job's turkey" and, having been raised in the country, "she knows good times and bad, quality folks and poor whites, Crackers and town folks. And good grief, what she doesn't know about negroes! She was raised up with them" and at the paper has become something of a specialist in "negro affairs," going to "colored graduations" and making sympathetic speeches. These words, and Myrick's writings from the set, convey precisely the paradoxical mixture of liberalism and paternalism of the would-be enlightened South of the time.

For Peggy, Susan became the perfect combination of adviser (coach and tutor to the actors), town crier, . . . and mole. Her experiences became fodder for dispatches to her newspaper, gossipy bulletins from the set that were a publicist's delight, extolling the charms of Gable and spinning his failure to achieve a Southern accent into earnest effort and success (it was a failure, and Gable soon wisely dropped it altogether). In her own diary and in her letters to Peggy Mitchell, she was more candid. In the diary she wrote, "Vivien is a bawdy little thing and hot as a fire cracker and lovely to look at. Can't understand WHY Larrie Olivier when she could have anybody." To Mitchell she described Olivia de Havilland in the childbirth scene, reading *Gone with the Wind* between takes of suffering and delivery. Peggy replied: "The picture of Melanie in labor, with 'Gone With the Wind' clutched to her and Scarlett anxiously cooling her brow, was wonderful. John [Marsh, Peggy's husband] says that the expression on Miss de Havilland's face is precisely the expression I wore during the time I was writing the book." With Myrick as her surrogate, Mitchell could thus maintain deniability while satisfying her craving to know everything.

■

All through 1938, Scarlett hopefuls came knocking at the house on Summit Drive, Selznick's home, and on the East Coast, Scarlett wannabes wrote, telephoned, rang the doorbell, and otherwise waylaid the embattled Margaret Mitchell. Southern aspirants threw themselves at Cukor, ambushed him on his trips to Georgia, besieged Margaret Mitchell until this normally polite woman had to stop answering the phone or giving interviews, cosh all invitations to draw her into speculations or preferences.

There was saturation coverage, "news" stories about every girl in Hollywood speaking with a Southern accent; every girl thinking she *was* Scarlett.

In its original planning, the Southern trip was to be headed up by Selznick, Cukor, and Kay Brown; it ended with Cukor and Brown going without Selznick. Canvassing had taken place of all the little theaters, while Washington and Lee and the University of Virginia had agreed to let candidates miss classes to get an audition. Part of this was marketing and PR—keep the South happy, but the South, not quite as dumb as it pretended to be, or as outsiders took it to be, began to sniff a con. Selznick memo'ed: "Because publicity has gone out thru the South calling Kay's trip a 'stunt,' idea is advanced that Cukor might sign one southern girl, to appear somewhere in the picture (Barbecue?) to prove our sincerity—or else to bring several southern girls to NY for auditions." Kay Brown wired back truculently that they were barricaded in their room after the open audition in Atlanta, which brought in five hundred contestants, "Every Miss Atlanta from 20 years back—how's you all, honey chile? We're done in!"

In the event, only ten girls looked remotely possible to Cukor, and only one made it all the way. Alicia Rhett wound up playing India Wilkes, joining Evelyn Keyes as a token Southerner. From Maine to Florida and from coast to coast, those on the sidelines were offering their casting choices to anyone who would listen. The conductor on the train in Clare Boothe Luce's satirical play *Kiss the Boys Goodbye* (1938) has his idea as to who should play

Scarlett. "Well," says he, "I got a preconceited notion . . . something half Hepburn, half Bette Davis, half Myrna Loy." "The failure to find a new girl is the greatest failure of my life," wrote Selznick.

Journalists did their bit to fan the flames ignited by studio publicity departments promoting one or another of their stars. Newspaper muckety-mucks like Ed Sullivan, Hedda Hopper, and Louella Parsons were dictating from their respective perches, resorting to blackmail when bullying wouldn't do. Sullivan attacked Selznick publicly for taking so long and, according to Selznick's laboriously detailed letter back, for "messing up *Gone with the Wind.*" This was September 1938, and Selznick, in a characteristically heated epistle that ran the gamut from scolding Sullivan to exhorting and appeasing him, made the inevitable point that since he hadn't made the film yet, he couldn't have botched it. He laid out all he felt he could disclose—quite a bit—regarding cast and crew. Of Scarlett, he writes, in his best *le public c'est moi* tone, "please believe me when I say that I have at my disposal more information as to whom the public wants in this picture than has anyone else. And the public's choice is clearly and very strongly for a new girl as Scarlett."

The self-anointed oracles pronounced on every candidate whose name emerged from the slush pile. About Tallulah Bankhead, Parsons wrote, "George Cukor, her friend, is going to direct, and Jock Whitney, another friend, is backing it. So I'm afraid she'll get the part. If she does, I personally will go home and weep, because she is not SCARLETT O'HARA in my language, and if David O. Selznick gives her the part, he will have to answer to every man, woman, and child in America." When the Englishwoman Leigh was cast, the crystal-gazing Louella prophesied that American audiences would boycott the movie en masse. In all fairness, she wasn't the only one to make such a prediction, especially when three of the four leads went to Brits. De Havilland had been born in Tokyo to British parents and only later became a naturalized American. She was at Warner Brothers, a studio notoriously reluctant to lend out its contract players. When Warner refused Selznick's entreaties, the smart and diplomatic actress, who would eventually fight her employer for better parts, took matters into her own hands. She invited her friend Ann— Mrs. Jack Warner—to lunch and made the case that playing Melanie would be a feather in the cap for both her and the studio. Ann was convinced and so, therefore and in due course, was Jack.

But one of the main reasons for Selznick's reluctance to buy the book in the first place was that he couldn't imagine who would play Scarlett, and from the beginning he felt it should be somebody new. This man who'd been in the business since he was a teenager loved casting and thinking about women, and knew instinctively the pitfalls of any choice, star, debutante, something in between. A newcomer wouldn't have the heft or experience (see the tests of a talented unknown named Edythe Marrener, soon to be known as Susan Hayward), while a star would have too much authority, be too inflexible and familiar a presence. Selznick didn't want the movie to be a star vehicle, a Bette Davis film or a Katharine Hepburn film. It was to be a David Selznick picture. It wasn't just the problem of an overweening personality but that a star would also be likely to change and shape or even dilute the part—Norma Shearer reportedly intended to make Scarlett more sympathetic. As he wrote in a memo to Cukor, who was doing screen tests (and was becoming more and more aggravated by Selznick's interference), he felt it would hurt the picture's draw to have "a girl who has an audience's dislike to beat down, as in the case of Hepburn [this was her 'box-office poison' period] or identification with other roles to overcome, as in the case of Jean Arthur." Only someone who had star quality, but didn't have an image of lovability to maintain, could do justice to the morally dubious heroine. Reciprocally, knowing that Selznick favored an unknown, the major actresses didn't want to test for the part, to put themselves forward and advertise their willingness only to be humiliated by failing to land it. As a cautionary example, Norma Shearer had undergone trial by fan club and been rejected for the part, and had made a very public withdrawal, holding a press conference, making a gracious concession speech, and saying, "I'd rather play Rhett."

Once a film becomes a classic, its cast seems so integral to its virtues one can't imagine how any alternative could have been considered, yet the paths to movies are far more arbitrary than their finished state might indicate. Even under the studio system, governed by a narrower, more efficient, and streamlined process, scripts might linger in the realm of dream and hypothesis, finagling and horse-trading, producers' heads filled with other casting choices who looked as interesting or even more promising (because better known) at the time. What if Howard Hughes had allowed Jean Simmons to play in *Roman Holiday*—would the incandescent sprite known as Audrey Hepburn ever have had the opportunity to capture our hearts? As much as we may love Jean Arthur as the secretary in *Mr. Smith Goes to Washington*, aren't we relieved she wasn't able to accept the role (Howard Hawks's first choice) in *His Girl Friday*? Or Ronald Reagan and Ann Sheridan in *Casablanca*? Casting is part of the writing, part of the adaptation. Even more to the point, what would *Gone with the Wind* have been like if Ellen O'Hara had been played by Selznick's first choice, Lillian Gish, rather than the more obscure Barbara O'Neil. (Barbara who? Exactly.) Gish would have brought stature and associations too vivid to die with her character's death, whereas O'Neil was perfect as the remote and deeply repressed mother, an idealized figure whose image fades when she disappears from the screen.

Evidence of the book's enormous and extremely special appeal to women was that every actress in Hollywood—and elsewhere—saw herself as Scarlett. Now that Vivien Leigh has imprinted her features on the part for all time, rendering the role unimaginable without her, we can only laugh at the contenders, the very idea of Katharine Hepburn or Norma Shearer. It's almost easier to start with those who weren't in the running, who were never considered. Marlene Dietrich ("She can't make people cry," Selznick wrote in a memo while making *The Garden of Allah*), Shirley Temple, Ginger Rogers, Judy Garland (though she was considered for the role of Carreen, the least important O'Hara girl), Asta, Lassie, Joan Fontaine (prepared for Scarlett; she came for an interview with Cukor and then found it was Melanie they had in mind, whereupon she is supposed to have turned up her nose and recommended her sister—a claim disputed by almost everyone).

The first three names bandied about came up just because they were Southern: Tallulah Bankhead, Miriam Hopkins, and Margaret Sullavan. There existed in the public mind a generic type of Southern bad-belle, professionally charming, narcissistic, her honeyed tones disguising the venom of a rattlesnake. The Virginian Margaret Sullavan as the antebellum flower of *So Red the Rose* was a "good" belle, hence the wrong type, too straightforward, too smart, too decent. And then there were those whose patrician breeding masked a taste for the gutter: Tallulah Bankhead, the wild and wellborn (and distinctly nonvirginal) Alabamian who had prevailed on her friend Jock Whitney to see that she was tested (a memo from Selznick, November 11, 1936: "Bankhead is first choice among established stars—and many votes coming in for her. She is taking Arden treatments and preparing for Cukor's arrival in NY to test her"). And Miriam Hopkins had played a genuwine Southern lady-trollop in *Sanctuary* (one of the films that had provoked the outrage that led to the Production Code). Hopkins had lent her claws and scheming ways to Becky Sharpe but was a little too old now for the seventeen-year-old seductress, her arch Southern charm a little shopworn.

Then there was that famous carpetbagger, Bette Davis from Lowell, Massachusetts, who through sheer willpower and ocular intensity was to become the best-known Southern belle of them all. In a sense, she'd unwittingly auditioned for the part as Dallas O'Mara (rhymes with guess what) in *So Big!* (1932) from the Edna Ferber saga; as a plantation owner's seductive daughter in 1932's *Cabin in the Cotton;* and as a Tex-Mex housewife in *Bordertown.* She was also an expert at bad girls and spinsters and would win an Oscar as a Southern rebel in 1938's *Jezebel.* Having flourished in bad-girl roles, she had the least to lose, the least distance to cover, in playing the bitch Scarlett. Not just Jezebel but later, the rapacious Sidney from Richmond in John Huston's *In This Our Life* (from the novel by another Southerner, Ellen Glasgow). But her wicked heroines are made to do penance, her pride bled out of her by forces natural and unnatural (the plague in Jezebel)—at least until the all-out evil of Regina (*The Little Foxes*) and malevolence of Baby Jane's sociopath sister. No question that Davis could play Southern and play mean; but truly bewitching? She was never a beauty or a glamour-puss femme fatale. Indeed, as an actress, she had made a career out of *not* being beautiful, as if plainness was morally superior to beauty and certainly more creditable to a thespian (a view generally shared by the Academy of Motion Picture Arts and Sciences). She defied you not to believe in her powers of seduction, and her costars supported this illusion, but would that be enough for Scarlett?

At whatever point she read the book and expressed a desire for the part (late, possibly never; there are conflicting versions), she definitely thought she should have been cast, that it was somehow hers by divine right. (This, although one version has her rejecting the role because Warner insisted she costar with Errol Flynn.) "Everybody's second cousin was tested," she wrote in her autobiography, *The Lonely Life*. "And I was used as the touchstone. That was how right I was. It was insanity that I not be given Scarlett, but then, Hollywood has never been rational."

Davis might have been led into believing the part was written for her by Margaret Mitchell's opening line, "Scarlett O'Hara was not beautiful, but men seldom realized it when caught by her charm as the Tarleton twins were." Bette Davis was not beautiful either, but that's a trope of Victorian novels that works only on the page—that is, the heroine whose beauty is not obvious (read: vulgar) but partially hidden, its secret available only to the discerning male (whose divination marks him as superior and worthy husband material)—and a sop, and breath of hope, for all of us nonbeauties. Movies have to go with the more superficial kind of beauty, though one possessed of some interesting quirk or imperfection. It's up to the actress to suggest plainness, awkwardness, severity, moments of nonbeauty. Plainness and awkwardness were simply beyond Vivien Leigh, but she wasn't afraid of looking haggard or grim, or suddenly older. Fear, fury, and the ravages of worry took her beautiful face into areas where beauty was irrelevant, charm repudiated. Her rage could be terrifying, indifferent to sex appeal, far from the arsenal of the femme fatale, yet somehow it was precisely the willingness of this beauty to give up her great asset that made those furrowed-brow moments of fear or displeasure strangely moving, even endearing.

There is also a necessary cinematic truth: Scarlett has to bewitch us at first sight and never let go. On the veranda with the Tarleton twins, two dazzling moments: the first as she teases her suitors, all girlish beauty and simpering charm-school flirtation; the second, after stricken by the news of Ashley's engagement, an almost unrecognizably altered young woman, standing in paralyzed horror, her green eyes widening and darkening with passion. Never underestimate the allure of those green eyes, but it's the quick succession of emotions that makes her entrance unforgettable. Contradicting her vaunted fearlessness, there's that element of fear in her reaction to the revelation—after all, if Ashley is not hers, then her romantic ideal, her very God, threatens to crumble. This is succeeded, split seconds later, by fear's antidote, the resolution to *do* something. In these first moments, we're being led subliminally to take a broad view of her. She is, unlike Mitchell's description of her heroine, outrageously beautiful, but in all other respects, the mixture of fineness and grit, the eyes of "pale green without a touch of hazel" and the "magnolia-white skin," she resembles the book's Scarlett. If her features have none of the heaviness of her Irish father's, they convey something spiritually akin: the toughness, the ability to run roughshod over and against the grain of other people's feelings. Mitchell describes "green eyes in the carefully sweet face . . . turbulent, willful, lusty with life, distinctly at variance with her decorous demeanor." Cukor later pointed to that as being Vivien incarnate, adding "She was Rabelaisian, this exquisite creature, and told outrageous jokes in that sweet little voice."

But Leigh had yet to make her entrance into David Selznick's life, and the popularity polls continued. At one point (July 1938) there were 300 votes for Ann Sheridan, 228 for Miriam Hopkins, 58 for Joan Crawford, and 61 for Katharine Hepburn, none of whom had done a screen test. At another time it was (1) Davis, (2) Hepburn, (3) Hopkins, (4) Crawford, (5) Margaret Sullavan, and (6) Barbara Stanwyck.

The idea of Hepburn as Scarlett seems ludicrous—"she lacked the sex element," as Selznick pointed out—and it's hard to imagine her New England forwardness and affected Brahmin accent eliding into flirtatious Dixie belle timbre. Yet there was a deeper kinship with the part that nobody realized, least of all the two women, and that might well have informed Hepburn's playing of the role. Born within seven years of each other, she and Mitchell were both the daughters of much-admired, if controversial, radical feminists, women whose actions and principles set a standard impossible for their less politically and academically inclined daughters to follow. Hepburn went fairly unwillingly to Bryn

Mawr and got suspended for smoking, though she eventually graduated; Mitchell went unwillingly to Smith and was secretly relieved to return home her freshman year.

In the style of many of their contemporaries—the equivalent of today's sex-and-the-city power women for whom "feminism" is a dirty word—they reacted to the "puritanical" self-importance of the previous era, becoming flappers and hell-raisers. Katharine Houghton Hepburn and May Belle Stephens Mitchell were hard acts to follow, and Hepburn and Mitchell, desperate for love, became attention-getting drama queens whose frivolity was a rebuke and whose accomplishments were a revenge. Almost everything the daughters did was in the long shadows of mothers whose love and respect they yearned for. If Hepburn was a front-runner for Scarlett, it was the triumph of sheer, brash I-can-do-anything egotism over sense or suitability.

Finally, toward the end, it was Paulette Goddard, close friend and neighbor of the Selznicks, who was the leading candidate, but she was also a scandal risk. Polls showed that women's clubs might not approve of her illicit relationship with Charlie Chaplin (though Selznick figured that if necessary he could get them to the church in time). Goddard, who'd played Ziegfeld and Goldwyn girls, with Chaplin's *Modern Times* her only starring role (she'd go on to play the memorably saucy divorcée in *The Women*), had the right amount of freshness, beauty, and spark. Yet her tests showed none of the spontaneity, the impishness, the personality she reveals in home movies except in a charming off-the-cuff moment where she's alternating between Mammy (whom she mimics wonderfully) and Scarlett. When she has to be serious, she suddenly looks "hard" (Cukor's word) with concentration, with the unnatural effort to be tight-lipped and scheming, not to be *nice*. In *The Women* she's the worldly one, more Scarlett than the others (Crawford's salesgirl being a low-rent Scarlett), but when the script (and screen test) of *Gone with the Wind* requires her to alter her naturally pleasing expression to one of narrow-eyed determination, she looks like a strained parody of the fierce, frightening glitter Leigh brings to such scenes.

In the final reckoning, the search ended up taking two years, costing ninety-two thousand dollars and involving consideration of some fourteen hundred candidates. Ninety of these took screen tests, with full-color tests for the four finalists: Joan Bennett, Jean Arthur, Paulette Goddard, and Vivien Leigh. Cukor chose the three sequences: the corset scene, Scarlett's attempted seduction of Ashley, and the moment after the war when she pleads with Ashley to run away with her.

As inconceivable as the film seems without Vivien Leigh, her arrival after the movie had begun shooting, her appearance on the set of a burning Atlanta, her sudden emergence before David Selznick with the flames of the "Depot" (an old movie set) behind her—is a "discovery" scene so fabulously right that someone would have had to invent it, and perhaps in part they did. Vivien Leigh had come from London to Los Angeles to join Olivier, who was preparing to make *Wuthering Heights*. She was hoping Olivier's agent, Myron Selznick, might arrange a meeting with his brother that would give her a crack at *Gone with the Wind*. Did David meet her before this fateful night? Possibly. What's beyond doubt is that it was December 10, 1938, the official beginning of the film, and the whole crew, invited guests, and hangers-on were gathered to watch the shooting of a scene (itself a stop-the-presses spectacle) that would be one of the film's most memorable—Scarlett and Rhett's flight from a burning Atlanta. All of the twelve available Technicolor cameras in Hollywood, along with the hoses of a sizable portion of the Los Angeles Fire Department, were trained on a row of old buildings (the *King Kong* set and others ready for striking) going up in flames. Against this backdrop Myron, accompanied by Larry and Vivien, greets his brother, makes introductions, and says, "Here's your Scarlett." Whatever they actually uttered ("I'll never recover from that first look," Selznick claimed he said), enough witnesses to the nighttime spectacle have confirmed Leigh's presence at this fortuitous moment, backlit by flames, watching as a stunt Scarlett and stunt Rhett, seen in silhouette, race in a buckboard to leave town before the fires devour them.

The fires somehow became an objective correlative for Vivien Leigh herself, her fierce temperament and ravenous desire for the part. She was "possessed of the devil," said Cukor, who adored her. So it's not surprising that her arrival wasn't quite the *dea ex machina* event favored by champions of the discovery myth, the fable in which a beautiful ingenue is plucked out of anonymity by a master Pygmalion and refashioned into a star. To begin with, she didn't just "happen" to be in LA because Olivier had to come for *Wuthering Heights*. She had paid her own way from London to California with the express purpose of meeting Myron, becoming his client, and enlisting his help in securing the role of Scarlett.

Born (in 1913) of Anglo-Irish parents in India, Vivian Mary Hartley had been brought up in convent schools and come out at Court before entering the Royal Academy of Dramatic Art to study acting and embark on a career on the stage. She had her first hit in 1935, in a play called *The Mask of Virtue*, a racy adaptation of Diderot's *Jacques le fataliste et son maître*, in which she showed her dual nature as a one-time prostitute masquerading as pure innocence. Not long before, she had seen Olivier perform and become obsessed with him, and when he saw her in *The Mask of Virtue*, he responded no less rapturously, writing in his memoirs, "Apart from her looks, which were magical, she possessed poise. . . . She also had something else: an attraction of the most perturbing nature I have ever encountered. It may have been the strangely touching spark of dignity in her that enslaved the ardent legion of her admirers."

Her theatrical career and their mutual passion took off from there; she did Shakespeare (playing Ophelia to Olivier's Hamlet), and the few negatives came from critics who disliked her voice or her limited vocal range. When Margaret Mitchell's book came out, she read it and immediately decided she wanted the part, asking her agent, John Gliddon, to submit her name to Selznick. At one point either Charles Morrison, Selznick's scout, or the ever-vigilant Kay Brown had alerted their boss to her talents, but Selznick apparently had not been overly impressed by her films— if he even had seen any. She's striking, but not dazzling, pretty in an exquisite Margaret Lockwood way. In three of some seven or eight early films, however, she shows minxlike sparks: in *Fire over England* (1937), as a lady-in-waiting to Queen Elizabeth I (Flora Robson), her rival for the love and loyalty of Olivier, as Michael Ingolby, who carries the queen's banner against the Spanish Armada; as the flirty adulterous wife of a bookstore owner in *A Yank at Oxford* (1938), where she has some charming scenes with Robert Taylor as the much-put-upon transplant (though Cukor remarked of her performance, "She seems to be a little static, not quite sufficiently fiery for the role"); and as a Cockney snitch who joins up with a group of buskers in 1938's *St. Martin's Lane* (aka *Sidewalks of London*), with Rex Harrison as her first prey and Charles Laughton as the poetry-reciting busker who shares his digs, and falls in love, with her. Her sweet little schoolgirl look when she first appears as a determined autograph seeker outside a theater encapsulates both the girlishness and the guile of the future Scarlett; the bookstore seductress shows her wiliness and flippant beauty; while her period lady-in-waiting is most Scarlett-like in the unladylike extremity and selfishness of her passion: she's someone who wants what she wants NOW and who doesn't believe in self-sacrifice for the cause. The sharp opposition between love (Leigh) and duty (Robson), between a glamorous inamorata in the service of a homely but stable lady monarch, eerily brings to mind that famous twentieth-century parallel, Lady Diana Spencer and Queen Elizabeth II.

It's easy to discover traits in hindsight, but the fact is, it's difficult to detect future stars. These are small films, and she remains small within them. The same is true of Audrey Hepburn in her British films or Ingrid Bergman and Greta Garbo in their Swedish films. These actresses hadn't yet had their eyebrows plucked, their teeth whitened and straightened, their breasts raised, their hairlines changed—in other words, been submerged in the Hollywood developing emulsion that raises star power to its full electromagnetic force. And more than the studio apparatus, they hadn't yet found the part and the director and the inner conviction that would transform them from minor beauties to space-devouring presences who, having learned how to be singularly, erotically, religiously alive in close-ups, the visual lexicon of stardom, would stop time and break down the two-dimensional barrier of the frame. There was something more than beauty in every case; in Leigh's, not yet apparent in her earlier performances, an intensity or—more singularly—the negative beauty of Scarlett, a Jekyll-and-Hyde mercurialism, the wide eyes narrowing into harsh willfulness. In the other screen tests— the best being Joan Bennett's and Paulette Goddard's—you understand the difference: Goddard can be pert, playful, even tough, but they seem to be discrete emotions, one ends, another begins, whereas Leigh's fluctuations—angry, saucy, coquettish, peevish, tragic—come rapidly, fluidly, coexist organically within the same volatile person. She also had the same French-Irish background as Margaret Mitchell.

In the days following that December night, tests were made, Leigh mastered the Southern accent in a matter of days, as if it had been an alternate personality waiting to emerge, and she won the part. She got out of the play she was to do with Michael Korda, left her husband and daughter dangling in England, sent a "Dear John" telegram dismissing her agent without a backward glance. She had married Leigh Holman, a barrister, when she was only nineteen and given birth to a daughter, Suzanne, within the year. Holman had never approved of her acting career, and now that Leigh was so deeply involved with Olivier, she had hoped for an annulment—yet she continued to write affectionate, wifely letters. With David Selznick, she showed her independence by demanding a shorter-term contract. Her leverage was her preference for the theater—the conventional snobbery toward movies—reinforced by her longing to work alongside the beloved and revered Larry. In truth, she was made for the movies, as Olivier never was, but *Gone with the Wind* was both the glorious peak and the beginning of the end of her movie career as a woman in full possession of her beauty.

But the twenty-five-year-old Leigh emerged in full flower before the camera when she made the screen tests for *Gone with the Wind.* The "paddock" scene in which she begs Ashley to run away with her has received a great deal of attention from critics because of the difference between the test—with a wooden Douglas Montgomery as Ashley—and the same scene in the film with Leslie Howard. Most have preferred the screen test, where the camera is trained on Leigh, and indeed, she is unforgettable: her mastery of the part, the Southern accent, combined with a bitter, weary maturity absent in any of the other candidates whose tests survive—it's easy to see why she was instantly chosen. Yet the scene with Howard is the finer one. The camera is set at a greater distance and a different angle that includes them both, making the scene more mutual and her role less domineering. In the screen test, she has a satanic, almost diabolical intensity, it's a one-sided (and suffocating) act of lovemaking as she importunes Montgomery, thrusts her body close to his, and initiates the kiss. In the better scene with Howard, there's more of an answering gaze.

In fact, we can see in the two tests the specter of a frighteningly out-of-control—or manipulative—Scarlett/Leigh that was part and parcel of her makeup, what critics have variously called her "neurotic desperation" or the "duality in her nature."

But she was still in the peaceful early days of the movie, working under Cukor, laughing about the fact that she had been competing for the part with actresses in costumes that were still warm from their bodies when she got into them. The real desperation came later in filming: weeks of separation from Larry (Selznick wouldn't let her leave often enough to visit him), the increasingly arduous shooting schedule, made more grueling by location work, and especially the firing of Cukor, which left her feeling devastated and abandoned. She wrote to Leigh Holman that her joy had gone out of the picture when Cukor left (though she continued to visit him on weekends for coaching sessions). Although she liked and was charmed by David, she couldn't depend on him to protect or defend her, and he in turn was taken aback at her aggressiveness on her own and the book's behalf ("Vivien's no Pollyanna," he said). She now had to go into battle for herself, much like Scarlett after the war was declared, and a battle of wills ensued between her and Victor Fleming. She infuriated him by bringing the book to the set and constantly referring to it, trying to introduce subtleties while the tough-guy director responded to her every request for help with a scene to just "ham it up!"

Toward the end of shooting, she was working a hectic eighteen hours a day, trying to finish so she could go back to Olivier. Their quickie weekends together were by all accounts frenzied sexual marathons, largely having to do with Leigh's unusually large appetites. From the early days in England, their relationship had always been consuming and physical. Reporters commented that even when their spouses were on the set, they had a hard time keeping their hands off each other, and now, in her rare breaks from *Gone with the Wind*, she and Olivier would spend the entire three days in a hotel room, ordering room service and locked in each other's arms, described in blunt, joyous, four-letter exclamations in her later account of the trysts.

Feeding into the intensity of her performance was not only the longing to get back to her lover but the feverishness of as-yet undiagnosed mental and physical illnesses, the manic-depression and tuberculosis that would begin to engulf her life almost as soon as the film was over. There were fits of hysteria and tears, yelling at Selznick in the way that she later would at Olivier during the tempests of psychosis that would cause havoc in the marriage, eventually ending it, and ruin her career. In and out of hospitals for shock therapy, subject to violent episodes that would force her to drop out of films, Leigh did indeed come to resemble one of the pitiable wreckages of womanhood she came to play. Yet unlike, say, the has-been actress she portrayed in the ghastly *Roman Spring of Mrs. Stone* (1961), a no-talent diva regarded as over the hill simply by virtue of being forty years old, Leigh was never without talent . . . or men.

Yet it was the affair with and marriage to Olivier that captured the public's imagination. While it lasted, at least in its early years, theirs was a love that, astonishingly, not only didn't handicap their careers but was granted dispensation from a usually censorious press and public. In 1939, when *Gone with the Wind* was shooting, they both had marriages back home, she a child, yet somehow the press treated them with kid gloves. Part of this can be attributed to the way studios controlled journalists much as the White House now controls the press corps, threatening to blackball them if unsavory "ink" was spilled. But this illicit couple was emanating its own magic aura. When *Wuthering Heights* opened that April, Olivier went from being a prestigious stage actor to an international star, and a Byronic one at that. (One can't help but imagine what it might have been with Leigh instead of Merle Oberon as Cathy!) "A Love Worth Fighting For" was the headline of a thorough and favorable piece on the couple by Ruth Waterbury that appeared in *Photoplay* in December 1939, in time for the premiere of *Gone with the Wind*. The tone, and therefore the public attitude, was set with this admiring description: "the high tumultuous romance that laughs at careers, hurdles the conventions, loses its head along with its heart, and laughs for the exhilarating joy of such wildness."

They combined breathtaking beauty with outsized gifts, he the lustrous prince of the theater, she the incandescent Hollywood star. Like Elizabeth Taylor and Richard Burton several decades later, they defied censure and brought together two worlds in mutually erotic stargazing. The difference was that Taylor, the established and much-married star, had no problem with her Hollywood credentials, whereas Leigh, younger and still a debutante, looked to Olivier to direct and define her career. Her first husband had disapproved of her acting; in deference to him she had briefly quit the stage but was drawn ineluctably back. Her life and vocation were in Olivier's hands, and the actor, himself insecure in Hollywood, wasn't all that devoted to her best interests. According to David Thomson, he even performed devious tricks to keep his first wife, Jill Esmond, and then Leigh, from getting parts that might eclipse him.

They had their one glorious cinematic moment together in *That Hamilton Woman* in 1941, just after their divorces were finalized and they were married (there's a scene in that movie where she seems to see the future, relinquishing him not verbally but with a sorrowful gaze into a lonely life). Leigh's other most memorable post–*Gone with the Wind* performance was in the wartime tearjerker *Waterloo Bridge* (1940), as the ballet dancer who falls in love with a naval officer (Robert Taylor) just as he's going off to war. In his absence she must take to the streets, but as she waylays soldiers at the train station, she still looks, titillatingly, like a schoolgirl who's gotten lost in the wrong section of town. Here in its most classic form is that ever-tantalizing contrast between the exquisite, well-bred ingenue and the tramp, the tart emerging from the kittenish demoiselle.

Spasmodic work during the war was followed by a series of theatrical successes in London and abroad, sometimes together with Olivier, sometimes with him directing her, as he did in the British production of *A Streetcar Named Desire* in 1949. Because she was always being compared with Olivier and lacked a strong voice, her theater work has been underrated. Yet her performances in such plays as George Bernard Shaw's *The Doctor's Dilemma*, Thornton Wilder's *The Skin of Our Teeth*, Jean Giraudoux's *Duel of Angels*, and Shakespeare's *Titus Andronicus*, as well as her two Cleopatras (Shaw's and Shakespeare's, alternating nights and aging twenty years) and her Lady Macbeth, dazzled critics and audiences alike.

But the cough and mood swings that had begun at the end of *Gone with the Wind* had become a huge concern, periodically disabling. There followed a miscarriage, depression, memory loss, hospitalizations and shock treatments, and, most unsettling, complete personality changes so that Leigh would become un-recognizable to her friends. Even when she seemed to recover her physical strength, she was subject to violent outbursts, claus-trophobic seizures in which she would tear off her clothes and slip into the character of Blanche DuBois. Blanche DuBois was itself a triumph of will and personality over native gifts. Director Elia Kazan, who started as a skeptic and ended in awe, found her an actress of "small talent, but the greatest determination to excel of any actress I've known." In a description so apt and vivid it's painful, he says in his autobiography that "she'd have crawled over broken glass if she thought it would help her performance."

Indeed, she practically did to get the part in the first place. People have speculated that Tennessee Williams had Leigh as Scarlett in mind when he wrote *Streetcar* and created the other great Southern belle of the twentieth century. The play/movie even seemed to be a Selznick family affair, David having discov-ered the actress who would come to play the heroine of the play produced by his (by then ex-) wife. But Lillian Gish, according to most sources, was the inspiration for the stage production. Leigh knew this but wanted the part so desperately that she engineered the London staging with Olivier directing — in effect, her (successful) audition for the film. Certainly there's a lot of Scarlett in Blanche, the Southern beauty cast back on her own fragile resources, a kind of faded black-and-white version of the robust Georgia peach, with Brando as a low-rent Rhett. Yet the differences are greater: Blanche is more deluded than the clear-eyed Scarlett, who, unlike Blanche, sees things as they are and never looks back, never yields either to nostalgia or to the temptation of vice. It's hard to imagine a Scarlett aging and unbeautiful (though as time went on, she might hit the brandy bottle a little more frequently) and equally hard to imagine the heroine without her signature gumption. Leigh herself may have started out as Scarlett, a canny self-promoter hiding behind the fragile beauty, but finally, and sadly, came more closely to resemble Blanche DuBois.

Unlike Olivier, who acted from the outside in, Leigh would *become* her parts, invest so much of herself in them that their trials would become her trials, their triumphs—and now increasingly their sufferings—hers. After *Streetcar*, Blanche DuBois would become the prototype of a string of fragile, if elegant fallen ladies she would come to play, increasingly pathetic, lonely, of a certain age, often Southern, frazzled by drink or delusion, such as Mary Treadwell, Southern lush, in *Ship of Fools* (1965). While in Ceylon in 1953, doing *Elephant Walk* (and having an affair with Peter Finch), she fell into several such episodes, eventually collapsing and having to quit working—to be replaced, ironically, by Elizabeth Taylor. Olivier, not always the most sterling character, had shown remarkable patience, but in 1960, they divorced.

When it mattered, Leigh's need to please the exalted Olivier and to earn the respect of his peers in the theater surely kept her from taking her movie career and her extraordinary gifts as seriously as she might have, and who knows how many opportunities—for her, and thus for us—were sadly missed. Yet as we watch her in *Gone with the Wind*, who can judge Olivier's influence as entirely baleful? Driven by that craving for Olivier's approval so central to her being, Leigh's performance expresses the whole crazy oxymoron of obsessional love, of Scarlett's for Ashley, of Leigh's for Olivier, of the fan's for his idol. All desire the impossible, to enter the body and spirit of that person, to be both consumed and made whole by him. Burnout was inevitable for this actress with her strange and unstable mixture of talent and beauty, who "gave so much more to the film than it ever gave back to her." But in this moment, her love for Olivier, both life-destroying and life-defining, was surely the catalyst for a performance worth a dozen Oscars from other actresses.

■

Despite her naïveté about the book-publishing world, Mitchell would prove as tough as Leigh in protecting herself with Macmillan and David Selznick. In another odd similarity with Leigh, she also depended greatly on her husband. John Marsh, former newspaperman, was not only her principal cheerleader and the final arbiter in the editing of her book but the husband she could feel comfortably dependent on, who would, in effect, allow her to maintain the image of a dutiful feminine wife. Other resemblances between the two women are also striking: she and Leigh were both *bien-elevées* debutantes with a ribald sense of humor, a salty tongue, and the spirit of the devil. Margaret Mitchell, who had herself gone through a chameleon phase in her debutante-flapper years, might have seen something of herself in Leigh when she wrote to Selznick, after Leigh's casting was announced, "I am impressed by the remarkable number of different faces she has. In the stills you have been good enough to send me, she looks like a different person every time she is shown in a different mood." And this just from black-and-white photographs!

And the actress who, on reading the book, wasn't just mad for the part but somehow *knew* it was hers, must have recognized the affinity when she wrote this telegram: DEAR MRS. MARSH: IF I CAN BUT FEEL THAT YOU ARE WITH ME ON THIS, THE MOST IMPORTANT AND TRYING TASK OF MY LIFE, I PLEDGE WITH ALL MY HEART I SHALL TRY TO MAKE SCARLETT O'HARA LIVE AS YOU DESCRIBED HER IN YOUR BRILLIANT BOOK."

Mitchell did support her, both publicly and privately, and the rest of the South eventually came round. Even the Daughters of the Confederacy, were, to Selznick's surprise, among the first on board: "Better an English girl than a Yankee," one of them had reasoned.

Eerily matching dualisms seem to play out in the uncanny fit of the trio of Selznick, Mitchell, and Leigh, each being possessed of fire-and-ice opposites that they projected into their lives and careers. Leigh, the mesmerizing mixture of bawdy sexpot and exquisite doll, echoed the Scarlett-Melanie sides of Margaret Mitchell, flapper turned matron. Mitchell, in turn, was attracted in fiction and in life to male opposites: the blackguard and the saint (she created one of each; she married one of each). Selznick, when he couldn't have Vivien Leigh for his protégée, turned to Jennifer Jones, the dark-haired Galatea who came to embody both wide-eyed innocents (*Since You Went Away*) and palpitating sexpots. These erotically charged heroines were, in turn, attracted to good boy–bad boy opposites: as half-breed Pearl, in *Duel in the Sun*, to Gregory "Love-'em-and-Leave-'em" Peck and Joseph "Mr. Sensitivity" Cotten or, as a strutting, pulpy Ruby Gentry, to swaggering Charlton Heston and sweet Karl Malden.

The intensely personal energy of this dividedness, the deep-down tension in Mitchell, Selznick, and Leigh between vulgarity and refinement, is what gives the archetypes in *Gone with the Wind* their extraordinary human resonance. So much of who these three were went into it, perhaps too much for the resumption of ordinary life. For both women, as for Selznick, the movie's success would be a severely mixed blessing. Selznick's sense that he knew it all now gave way to a megalomania that knew no bounds; nothing could equal the success of his "masterpiece," yet (with the financial carelessness of his father) he wound up losing the lion's share of the profit in an obligatory liquidation of his company. As for the two women, the fame and acknowledgment they sought was also a curse, the effort itself—nine years for Mitchell, a seven-month lifetime for Leigh—were a strain of monstrous, life-shortening proportions. Would either have had it otherwise? Possibly. Leigh died after a recurrence of tuberculosis in 1967; she was fifty-three. The accident-prone Mitchell was forty-nine when, on her way to a movie, she walked into the path of an oncoming taxi. David Selznick was in a court battle over rights to *Gone with the Wind* when he died in 1965 at the age of sixty-three.

THREE

Finding the Road to Ladyhood Hard

A child of the century, Margaret Mitchell was born in November 1900—quite literally in the backyard of the Civil War. The battle had ended only thirty-six years before she was born, and its remnants—those ghostly Confederate entrenchments at the bottom of Jackson Hill—could still be seen from her grandmother's house. That would be Annie Fitzgerald Stephens, real-life progenitor of Scarlett and mother of Mary Isabelle "May Belle" Stephens Mitchell. On the porch of her old Victorian mansion, which had been left miraculously intact when Sherman's troops swept through a burning Atlanta, Margaret heard stories of uncles and grandfathers who'd been radical secessionists, brigands, spies, often from the lips of the patched and wounded veterans themselves. In later years, she claimed that it wasn't until she was ten that she realized the South had lost the war. Out on the Jonesboro Road, her grandmother's farm, the Fitzgerald place—the inspiration for Tara—still stood erect, though Sherman's army had laid waste its fields. In Grandmother Stephens's back lot, she and her neighborhood pals reenacted the Civil War with their own versions of the famous battles. At night, in the Mitchells' house nearby, May Belle sang Negro spirituals and ballads to put her daughter to sleep, and one of them, "Tote the Weary Load," almost became the title of the book.

Awesome May Belle, high-minded, an intellectual, is the activist out of whom Ellen O'Hara was born. But Scarlett's immediate model was the no less awesome and frequently appalling Annie. The maternal grandmother was a tough, conniving busybody who survived the war along with her property and made a fortune in real estate afterward. A staunch Roman Catholic, this imperious and powerfully divisive woman made Margaret's life miserable after May Belle died. Neither mother nor grandmother possessed any maternal warmth, but whereas Annie had simply dispatched her large brood of children to be raised by relatives, May Belle took over her son and daughter's upbringing with a zealous hand and, where Margaret was concerned, an acute ambivalence. May Belle was determined her daughter would do everything a boy could do: by the time she was six, Margaret could ride a horse and shoot a rifle, but she was forced by her mother to take lessons in dance and deportment. Being a tomboy was second nature; being a lady was not.

Later photographs of the young Margaret Mitchell are a study in contrasts: see her as, respectively, Jazz Age deb and married lady. In the former, aged about nineteen, she poses provocatively in a low-cut ball gown, her flat flapper bosom thrust slightly forward, a flower behind her ear, a come-hither look in her teasing eyes. In the latter, fifteen years later, she's sitting at a desk in a demure polka-dot dress, white collar and cuffs, the quintessence of matronliness, "mature lady with manuscript," with the accent on lady. What we can't see is that the lady who loved to dance is now wearing orthopedic shoes. It's as if she's fulfilled the nightmare vision that horrified Scarlett at the Twelve Oaks barbecue—spirited belles in beautiful dresses dancing the night away and, on the sidelines, the chaperones, many of them no older than the belles, cast into social Siberia by marriage and dowdy at twenty. Scarlett has seen the future in the starkest possible terms ("Married women never had any fun"), and she wants no part of it. Mitchell first resisted, then burrowed into it.

The dividedness suggested by the pictures was perhaps not quite pathological, but it was certainly the motif that cleaved Mitchell's sensibility and inspired her art. There was the flapper against the little woman (Scarlett versus Melanie), the lowbrow (Mitchell) versus the highbrow (her mother), or the near-illiterate Scarlett versus the intellectual Ashley, the pagan versus the Christian. . . . And there are intricate permutations of rebellion, as May Belle, the activist mother, fought for women's rights, a cause Margaret never overtly espoused but one that permeated her work in oblique and instinctual ways. Mitchell makes us feel a helpless ambivalence before the conundrum of Scarlett, the woman who became the heroine almost against her author's wishes. An unlikely heroine, even an unwanted one, and here may be the source of her staying power—we move in to fill the gap of sympathy withheld by her creator. And if we stay with her long past ordinary human forbearance, it's that we feel behind her desperate maneuvers the cry of a lost child: those recurring nightmares, the terror of abandonment, the feverish search for security, and, underlying all and paramount, the longing for a mother.

A key moment comes almost halfway through *Gone with the Wind*, book and movie, when Rhett abruptly abandons Scarlett on the road to Tara to join the Confederate army. With Melanie, her baby, and Prissy in the back of the wagon, they've gotten through the hellfire of a burning Atlanta, Rhett beating back scavengers who try to steal *his* stolen nag, and are finally on the Jonesboro Road, when he announces that he's going to join "the brave lads in gray." He and Scarlett have just watched as a dying and defeated army passes them, straggling back to town. As usual, she misreads his emotions, fails to see the spark of sympathy for the formerly "swaggering" and "boasting" troops. Still, nothing prepares us for this showdown when he forsakes Scarlett in the name of a higher integrity, one to which he had shown little previous allegiance, and consigns her to a possibly suicidal journey through Union territory and to a self-reliance she has never desired. His desertion follows hard upon one of their tenderest scenes together, when, finding her exhausted and terrified after Melanie's agonizing delivery and determined to get back to Tara, he holds and comforts her in the manner of the mother she longs to return to—or the mother she never had.

In attempting to explain Rhett's change of heart, which had a bevy of screenwriters gnashing their teeth, Sidney Howard et al. decided to translate *their* bafflement into Rhett's, having him puzzle over his own motives. "I always had a weakness for lost causes once they're really lost," he offers, or alternatively, "maybe I'm just ashamed of myself." In some ways it's the inexplicability of the act that marks it as deeply personal, springing from some demons of the unconscious on Mitchell's part, a prompting of the past rather than a rational plot calculation. But nothing comes out of *nowhere*. The scene is powerful precisely because it gives off glints of large, unseen forces, a Rosebud moment that makes sense only in retrospect. Even as he declares his love most passionately, one of Rhett's feet is pointed homeward, toward Charleston and the clan of bluebloods that will claim him in the end—his desertion of Scarlett the first revelation of a deep temperamental divide between the couple that bodes ill for any kind of "happy ending."

Rhett's withdrawal of those protective arms, and the chasm that suddenly opens up, reaches back to the turning point of Margaret Mitchell's own young life. "Stunned, nauseated" by Rhett's abandonment, the book's Scarlett compares it to a moment of terror when as a child of six she fell out of a tree and endured the frightening near-death sensation of having the wind knocked out of her. This was precisely the age when Margaret had her own expulsion from Paradise. It was September 1907; Margaret had begun school and hated it. Unpopular, resistant to anything "academic," and forced to exchange her boy's pants for a dress, she pleaded with her mother to let her quit. May Belle said not a word, but she had the carriage brought round and took the would-be truant for a ride north of Atlanta, in the open country on the famous road to Jonesboro. Here on land that still lay fallow years after the war stood many grand old mansions now derelict, tenanted by impoverished widows and spinsters. Margaret imagined these antebellum ghosts peering through cobwebbed windowpanes, Miss Havershams haunting the present day. This is what can happen, Mrs. Mitchell admonished her daughter, if you don't prepare. The world can go mad in an instant, crumble around you overnight.

"For God's sake, go to school and learn something that will stay with you," Margaret later quoted her mother as saying. "The strength of women's hands isn't worth anything, but what they've got in their heads will carry them as far as they need to go." This is the conversion narrative of Margaret's life, her Saul on the Road to Damascus peripeteia, only instead of finding Christianity on the road to Jonesboro, she learned a lesson in brute survival. Gumption would be her byword, not the grace of the Lord. And for Scarlett, not Christian forbearance but action and self-interest. This story achieved mythic proportions for

Mitchell—she recounted it often and to everyone as a message of inspiration—yet emotionally, it was one of desolation and withdrawal. And as an intellectual call to arms, it stalked and oppressed her, holding her to a higher standard than she believed she could ever fulfill.

The mother-daughter pep talk was her Rubicon: on one side, untroubled youth; in the aftermath, a girl with a precocious sense of responsibility and the need to measure up. The moment acquired a wealth of multilayered meanings—a loss of innocence, a call to independence, a feeling of insecurity and abandonment, a terror of winding up poor and alone, a beckoning to wider horizons—all of which fed into that other Rubicon on the road to Tara.

Like Scarlett's fall from the tree, Mitchell's childhood fall from a horse and the preposterous number of falls, injuries, illnesses, accidents, hospitalizations, depressions, and losses that followed—including May Belle's death from influenza when Margaret was eighteen—gave her life a sense of psychological peril. The self-destructive pattern beneath the superhuman effort of writing *Gone with the Wind* speaks of compensation for an abiding ache that, like Scarlett's yearning for home and mother, are somehow illuminated in that stern repudiation on the road to Jonesboro. In a moment that metaphorically encapsulates many others, we feel the daughter's failure to receive that most prized gift, unconditional love. The fall, the tumble into a void, the mother (preoccupied with worthier causes), saying, "Pull your-self together, you're on your own." Hence the lifelong insecurity beneath a veneer of bravado.

For Scarlett, there's one last chance at security, at changing the course of events. In the book, Rhett orders her roughly out of the carriage even as he declares passionate love, while she repeats to herself the mantra of the abandoned child, "He's leaving me, he's leaving me!" For the movie, William Cameron Menzies once again supplies the visual equivalent of fire and desperation. No rosy glow but flames redden the sky behind a Gable, towering in shirtsleeves and manly disarray, the equivalent of some of Mitch-ell's most overheated prose ("the hard muscles of his thighs against her body"), as the departing warrior demands a farewell kiss (something more in the book).

The request, given the circumstances of his desertion, is not a little outrageous . . . on the other hand, he *could* well die. When she holds back, he grabs her out of the buckboard and pulls her to him caveman style. She begins to respond but backs off as sanity returns. Or is it sanity? If she had responded in kind, her life—and *Gone with the Wind*—might have been a more conventional story, Scarlett a less radical figure. She would know in the "deep down" way of the romance heroine that, whatever the hard-ships, the handsome rescuer would be lurking in the wings. Her struggle to save Tara would be undercut and cushioned by the knowledge (ours, hers) that she doesn't really have to go it alone, that love in the form of Rhett's strong arms and practical sense would make everything right. Instead she refuses, or Mitchell refuses her, this solace.

Tara, unlike Twelve Oaks, still stands, but the Yankees have made off with everything usable, edible, or potable: animals, food, rugs, the wherewithal to survive . . . and Ellen is dead, laid out on a bier, cold and marmoreal. We think back to the time when young Scarlett, thunderstruck by the news of Ashley's engagement, wants desperately to talk to her mother, but Ellen arrives late for dinner and preoccupied from tending the Slatterys, and immediately afterward forms the family prayer circle. Religion, like mother, is cold comfort. And now, once again she's not there, this time literally, when her daughter most needs her. And Gerald—in a more extreme version of Margaret's own father, who doted on her mother and was inconsolable without her—has lost his mind.

When Pork and Mammy have itemized each fresh disaster, when the impact of their situation is borne upon her, Scarlett's whole body and demeanor change. Leigh makes the flirt and charmer disappear before our eyes; the belle's musical voice lowers several registers into a numb monotone. As in some fish species, when the school is deprived of its males, a female takes on the role of leader and actually acquires male characteristics, so the masculinized Scarlett of the post-war is born. The woman who wanted nothing more than a shoulder to lean on has become, by default, the mainstay, the authority figure upon whom others must lean.

Mitchell professed surprise that people saw Scarlett as the heroine, a role for which she had intended Melanie. Indeed, she could hardly explain the way Scarlett took over the book, as if some unconscious compulsion had drawn her demonically onward. Always concerned—at least post–*Gone with the Wind*—with retaining her credentials and friends as a Southern lady in good standing, she made a nominal apology to unnamed kibitzers who had "chided" her "for drawing a 'bad woman,'" saying she did not mean to "cast aspersions on all Southern ladies," nor did she "wish to embarrass anyone by making it appear they had a kinswoman of the type of Scarlett O'Hara." Was this disingenuousness? It seems more probable that she actually started out to write a story of Melanie, and Scarlett simply pushed her way to the forefront with an animal vitality that would not be denied. How did Mitchell create her in the first place—what influences did she draw on, and then, what possessed her to leave her alone, abandon her to her fate with a strange detachment that may be the true source of the story's staying power?

Where did this creature come from, self-willed, vain, and obstinate, yet more valiant than a general? A predator who marries three men she doesn't love (one of them, stolen from her sister, is later killed protecting Scarlett's "honor"), a rotten mother, though she never pretends otherwise. And the movie spares us the worst of it. Of her three offspring, only Bonnie Blue Butler, the last and most loved, makes it into the film. Merely a schemer and liar before the war, Scarlett takes a darker turn toward avarice and greed as she does what she must to survive . . . and more. A successful businesswoman, she defies decorum at every turn, hires and abuses convicts, consorts with Yankees and scalawags, flies in the face of every rule and instinct governing the behavior of decent women. On the asset side, there's her willingness to get down on her hands and knees in the dirt to save Tara and her entire household, her business acumen—that unfeminine knowledge of mortgages (if women today understood them as Scarlett did, there wouldn't be so many on the street!) and her success in the lumber trade—the "sexlessness" that shocks her community now seen almost as virtues to modern-day audiences. She despises hypocrisy, takes the blame for her mistakes, refuses the comfort of nostalgia and all the self-serving myths the South holds so dear. With her intimidating boldness (she tells Rhett she doesn't need him to rescue her), she seems to lose her Southernness altogether and to resemble nothing so much (horrors!) as a Yankee girl! There are even the occasional spasms of remorse, though these issue less from a chastened heart than from a fear of the Almighty's retribution, and finally even that fear fades. She has harbored so many hateful wishes and hurled so many spiteful curses and survived (as have the objects of her curses) that "God did not frighten her anymore."

But the real wonder in that catalog of sins, which surely outnumber and outweigh the virtues, is how little Scarlett pays for her wickedness in the patented forms of punishment. These would normally involve one or more of the following: sexual and psychological humiliation; a barrage of self-satisfied diatribes and blandishments from the people she's wounded; death or, in its stead, an eleventh-hour reversal whereby she repents of her wicked ways, is brought back to heel, and is transformed by love into a submissive female. Bette Davis, for example, as New Orleans's most scandalous debutante in *Jezebel* does penance and then some for arrogant and unladylike behavior. "Nussin' a spite" against beau Henry Fonda, she wears harlot red to the ball (anticipating Scarlett's not-so-grievin' widow dancing with Rhett at the bazaar in *Gone with the Wind*), whereupon she loses Fonda (to a Yankee lass, no less), sinks into isolation and depression, reforms her spoiled-brat persona, and, finally, when Fonda contracts the yellow fever (a disease with which she, as the embodiment of virulent nature, is slyly equated), accompanies him with the other afflicted and dying to the island of quarantine. As for Scarlett, yes, she is rejected, even briefly humiliated, by Rhett's indifference—but does that turn her into a "better" or different person? Less selfish? More spiritual? Hardly. The redemption of self-sacrifice is not an option: she revives, shrugs it off in her inimitable way, moves into forward gear with that instinct for survival that is so relentless and all-powerful it sometimes makes her appear more animal than human.

Rhett, dashing and mysterious, is or would seem to be the archetypal bad boy, but Scarlett is the real rogue, even calls herself one. In the end, Rhett plans to return to Charleston, and make his peace, a black sheep reformed, while no such penitential conformity can be expected from Scarlett. As a character she gets away with it in a way that is rare, not to say unprecedented in movies, given a double standard that generally grants such immunity only to the male of the species, the charismatic gangster, the bad boy beloved of women who should know better. It's not that she's completely unpunished: she loses Rhett, Ashley, Melanie, mother and father, almost everyone and everything, but she gets away with it as a character with whom the audience—most of it—forms a forgiving bond.

What about literary models? Most viewers and reviewers saw in her the Great Victorian Adventuress Becky Sharp. Mitchell insisted she hadn't read *Vanity Fair*, and it's possible she hadn't: William Thackeray's venal temptress and amoral seductress is wittier and more genuinely worldly than Scarlett, but the resemblances are too striking to disregard. They both have something more important than "mere" (that is, sheer, statuesque) beauty: an awareness of limitations and a strategic deployment of assets; each cannily lowers her eyes in a simulation of modesty then flashes them upward with devastating results. Then there's the contempt for other women, especially the idiot wellborn, whom each thinks her own cleverness gives her the right to shove aside in a deserved ascendancy over them; the way Becky or Scarlett can shape her chameleon personality to fit the occasion or the prey; the adaptability of each woman as war profiteer and ruthless bargainer; and most shocking of all, the utter lack of maternal feelings. Both treat their offspring as afterthoughts, nuisances best left to the care of others who have nothing better to do than devote themselves to such a distasteful task. Last, despite authorial protests on both counts, each rises to the status of heroine through sheer indomitability. The parallels between Becky and Scarlett might simply be that two fiddle-de-dee sort of girls (an expression they both use) were terrorists waiting to take advantage of particularly fatuous societies, just as Anita Loos's Lorelei Lee captured a moment when gentlemen were making fools of themselves over dumb blondes, only nobody had quite had the wit to call their bluff. Becky, of course, has a more finely etched satirical purpose. Thackeray, unlike Mitchell, is essentially a caricaturist and satirist, with the result that Becky and Amelia are less "rounded" than Scarlett and Melanie. Becky, moreover, is associated with the enemy Napoleon, the Corsican upstart, whereas Scarlett, however irreverent, is still allied with the "good" side in the Civil War. Yet both expose and parody the hypocrisies of an Old World class system through a different and more obvious sort of vanity.

And what are we to make of the comical moment at the Twelve Oaks barbecue (not in the movie) when Scarlett, eavesdropping on Melanie and Ashley, is delighted (if disconcerted) to hear, instead of sweet nothings, a "literary" conversation, as Melanie's sweet voice says, "I fear I cannot agree with you about Mr. Thackeray's works. He is a cynic. I fear he is not the gentleman Mr. Dickens is." Who's speaking here? Mitchell, her mother, or the Southern community, perhaps the Atlanta literary women's group that May Belle spearheaded, whose members might have taken offense at Thackeray's more pointed exposé of the *haute bourgeoisie?* The novelist's affectionate irreverence when it comes to women may have especially nettled them, his blurring of the line between virtue and vice, his witty provocations and improprieties, all cloaked in a highly ironic kowtowing to received opinion. Dickens might lament social inequities with passion and vigor, render unforgettable the horrors of poverty, but he genuflected before the virgin doll-woman!

Thackeray paves the way for Scarlett by challenging the Victorian convention whereby the virtuous woman is by definition the heroine. The great satirist asks us not so much to withhold moral judgment as to allow it to coexist with a more realistic admiration for qualities (Becky's Napoleonic resourcefulness and tactical genius) that men are given medals for. Is it possible that Melanie, for all her apparent dimness, sensed that Thackeray is at his sliest and most subversive when purporting to extol the virtues of the good-hearted but sappy Amelia, Victorian masochist par excellence? Not for Becky the "gentle martyrdom" and "tender slavery" of Amelia, not for Scarlett the sweet refinement of long-suffering Melanie.

Becky is genetically closer to Scarlett than, say, Emma Bovary, another possible prototype, also deceitful and vain, but gumptionless; Undine Spragg in Edith Wharton's *Custom of the Country* (more symptom than character); or Gwendolyn Harleth in George Eliot's *Daniel Deronda*, perhaps the grandest vixen all, but too multifaceted in a way, too fine and too victimized.

What about movies and the female swaggerers of her era? Roger Ebert, in an appreciation of the film on its fiftieth anniversary, suggests that Scarlett "is not a creature of the 1860's but of the 1930's, a free-spirited, willful modern woman," and traces her influences to frankly sexual movie stars like Clara Bow, Jean Harlow, Louise Brooks, and Mae West. Modern Scarlett surely is, but thirties she isn't. Clara Bow and Louise Brooks as silent film stars, possibly, but by 1930 and the advent of sound, Mitchell had essentially finished writing the book. Although she wouldn't surrender the manuscript until 1935, she spent those five years revising, correcting, fact-checking, and dithering. Because the book came out in 1936, the movie in 1939, it is forever associated with the thirties, especially since it seemed to connect so strongly with audiences as a Depression fable. But Margaret's associations were from the teens and twenties. The sexy pre–Hays Code stars Ebert refers to are subtly wrong as inspirations for Scarlett, who, like Mitchell herself, is far more ambivalent about sex. Which is why, though she might seem at first glance to point to the noir femmes fatales of the forties, she's not of their dark design, either. Unlike the femmes fatales of literature and film, generally the projection of male fantasies, Mitchell sees sexual attractiveness as a weapon but sex itself as something only men enjoy, hence a surrender on the part of women, even an enslavement. The authentically bad heroines, such as Jane Greer in *Out of the Past* and Barbara Stanwyck in *Double Indemnity*, are, unlike the chaste Scarlett, sexual predators, their charms deployed to nefarious, even homicidal ends. Not only is Scarlett repelled, her horror of sex is virtually a defining characteristic. When she feels Rhett's eyes undressing her in that first sighting at Twelve Oaks, her guard is immediately up. Her attraction is both triggered and chilled by her terror of sex, a function of her awesome pride and a very American need to stay in control. Her fantasy of being overpowered, like that of being "taken care of" by Ashley, are the longings of a woman exhausted by her own strength, beset by a fear of losing her femininity, hence her desirability. She has more in common with the heroines of screwball comedy than with the more overtly sexy pre–Hays Code babes or the sultry sisterhood of the forties. Words, threats, and smiles are her weapons of choice. When she comes to Rhett in prison in her plush green curtain dress, the sexual masquerade she performs for the saving of Tara is exposed by her dirty fingernails and rendered poignantly absurd by Rhett's laughter of recognition. Yet even here she refuses to be touched by Rhett's longing or, later, drawn into a playful communion. Marriage can be fun, he says, expressing the holy anthem of screwball. "Marriage *fun?*" replies a disbelieving Scarlett. She's not buying.

■

This intense resistance to the idea of marriage along with a knee-deep immersion in tales of war are both the leitmotifs and the framing context of Scarlett's terrors and triumphs, a projection of Mitchell's own preoccupations and dividedness. Her childhood was intertwined with the war to a degree that was extreme, if not unique, reinforced by the terrific racial strains of Atlanta, where local incidents and horrors seemed to bleed directly from war and Reconstruction. Though they never acquired quite the same mythic status as the road-to-Jonesboro episode, the terrifying Atlanta race riots of 1906 occurred virtually in the Mitchells' backyard when Margaret was five and her mother was away. The causes were complex—for one thing, the burgeoning Negro population, having gone from nine thousand in 1880 to thirty-five thousand in 1900, was straining city resources—but it was rumors of rape (white leaders falsely reporting attacks by black men on white women) that fired up white mobs, who roamed the city seeking and killing black victims. For three days gunshots rang out as violence from the adjacent Negro neighborhood, the white gangs, and the militia spilled into Jackson Hill. Probably one of the few homeowners without firearms, Eugene Mitchell stood guard with an ax until Margaret reminded him of the family sword. Little Margaret was seeing plenty of action and disaster in her short life, all of which would be stored away for future use. The famous Atlanta fire of 1917 also affected Jackson Hill. It started in the Negro section at the bottom of the hill when an old storage depot being used by a hospital caught fire, raged out of control, and spread, burning houses and taking lives. Teenage Margaret went to help at the refuge center, where the sight of burn victims moaning and lost children screaming made an indelible impression.

Atlanta's trials by fire, and its amazing survival, were coming to occupy pride of place in the heart of the girl who was discovering her inborn gifts as raconteur, dramatist, and impresario. She told ghost stories that made her pals' hair stand on end and wrote Westerns and Civil War plays, occasionally borrowing from such then-popular Southern authors as Thomas Dixon, the racist-evangelist author of *The Clansman* (the novel on which *Birth of a Nation* is based). Her stories were by all accounts remarkable for their narrative vigor and precocious sense of plot, as well as for their challenging and parodying of gender roles. If Margaret played the "cowboy hero" or soldier rescuer instead of the damsel in distress, she came by it naturally. Not only had her mother encouraged her in this, but at age six, she had regularly gone out riding with a pack of grizzled war veterans, had enjoyed being "one of the guys." At eleven she sustained her first riding accident and the ankle injury that would plague her life in one form or another. She was already a tomboy, having taken to wearing boy's clothes from the tender age of three when, in her first accident, her dress caught on fire (thanks to the carelessness of brother Stephens, who was watching over her!). The perils of femininity thus confirmed, she exchanged skirts for pants and rechristened herself Jimmy. But "Jimmy" was also subject to the authoritarian strictures of May Belle's Southern Lady side: dancing lessons and classes in deportment and decorum were obligatory and the bane of Margaret's existence.

The heavy foot of parental law came down in a particularly

crushing manner one day when Margaret and her all-female theatrical troupe, dubbed the "Sewing Circle," were performing a
scene from Margaret's dramatization of Thomas Dixon's *The
Traitor: A Story of the Fall of the Invisible Empire.* Margaret, with
slicked-back hair and wearing a fedora, about fifteen at the time,
was playing the protagonist and about to be hanged when interrupted by her mother and father, the copyright lawyer. They
gave her such a lecture on infringement of copyright that "for
years afterward," she later wrote, "I expected Mr. Thomas Dixon
to sue me for a million dollars, and I have had a great respect for
copy-right ever since then."

More than respect. She was possessed of a fear bordering
on mania of accidentally lifting, or being accused of lifting, someone else's prose. It was why—or so a number of people have speculated—that whenever she was asked if Scarlett had been influenced by Becky Sharp, she denied having read Thackeray's
Vanity Fair. In fact, she would tell correspondents the story of
how she'd avoided it. Thinking her daughter's literary tastes friv-
olous, May Belle had bribed her to read the classics: "a nickel for
Shakespear," she later wrote, "a dime for Dickens, 15 cents for
Nietzsche and Kant and Darwin." Her mother, she claimed, had
paid her fifteen cents to read *Vanity Fair,* but she couldn't get
through it. Only much later, in her account—long after *Gone
with the Wind*—did she read it . . . and love it.

By this time, the family had left Jackson Street, with its vast
backyard for riding and theatricals, to live in a huge, white-

columned house built, at May Belle's insistence, on an undeveloped stretch of the more fashionable Peachtree Street. An altruist much given to worthy causes, the mother with "belle" in her name was no less of a social climber for that, and the upgrade, with its fifty-foot facade and Palladian entrance, was her dream house of a Plantation, showier than its neighbors and beyond the family's means. (It was, in its own way, as vulgar as the Tara that David Selznick built in Hollywood, ironically the very aspect of the film Margaret denounced most loudly and repeatedly.)

They were Irish Catholic—and on her mother's side, devotedly Catholic. And though her ancestors were superior to the rough-and-ready O'Haras—they had included political leaders and entrepreneurs—the Mitchells were still not quite top-tier Atlanta WASP society, the judges, governors, and bishops of the Old Families at a time when society defined itself by the narrowest and bluest of bloodlines.

For the most part, class differences and class insecurity, which played such a large part in Mitchell's life and in the book (where questions of breeding and bloodlines are frequently discussed), get only a cursory airing in the movie. At the Twelve Oaks barbecue, the book's Scarlett observes the confidence of the girls who harbor "no such conflict as . . . raged in Scarlett's bosom where the blood of a soft-voiced overbred Coast aristocrat mingled with the shrewd, earthy blood of an Irish peasant." Yet even without these finer points being spelled out in the film, it's astonishing how much of this social anxiety and resentment Vivien Leigh conveys and how that very outsider status—with which we all identify—binds us to her even as the movie seems to celebrate the Old Order. She speaks to the raging conflicts in every young lady who wants to appear a "delicate and high-bred lady with boys and to be, as well, a hoyden who was not above a few kisses."

Nor does the quandary over how much a girl should "put out" without losing her reputation belong to ancient history. The difference between our single girls and theirs is that pleasure, in the earlier and chaster games based on flirtation, was more evenly distributed between the sexes. If anything, the girls had the power to say "no," and hence as "deciders" had the better hand.

Though Eugene Mitchell was neither a ruddy Irishman nor an aristocrat, he was not successful enough to support his wife's social ambitions. May Belle's father, Margaret's grandfather, had the distinguished mind in the family. When May Belle was at finishing school, he wrote long letters encouraging her to read and think, not to waste her time on escapist reading, and to practice the classical and manly virtues of courage, bravery, and daring. But—this practically in the same breath—also to take her place in the womanly sphere, where, in Victorian tradition, the woman was still the "Guardian Angel" and should "remain a little girl in feeling."

Social tensions along with the Mitchells' wildly conflicting attitudes toward the female of the species, Southern subset, may have presented Margaret with special difficulties. In any case, as a young girl, she'd never quite fit in, hadn't been popular, which, for a Southern female, is an affliction worse than a physical deformity. Her brother, Stephens, recalled that at her prep school, Washington Seminary, she made enemies and incurred bitterness that lasted throughout her life. During all those childhood activities, she'd been more of a tomboy than the other girls and a bit of a bully, too. To escape the impositions of gentility—the equivalent of Scarlett's hated corset—she wrote action stories, in one of which a heroine named Peggy faces down the Mexican bandit who has slaughtered her family. The scene sounds like a dry run for the one in which Scarlett takes aim at the Yankee intruder. "With infinite care Peggy slid the gun up to the level of her eyes and found the man across the sights. Coldly, dispassionately, she viewed him, the chill steel of the gun giving her confidence. She would not miss now—she would not miss—and she did not." The gun-toting Peggy, we might note, introduces her pseudonym, and prefigures the name Pansy, which is what the heroine of *Gone with the Wind* was called before she became Scarlett. With all this talent and energy came a bossiness that alienated her from her classmates.

At Smith, which she attended at May Belle's insistence, she was no less miserable. Margaret might rebel by reading trashy novels and acting up, but on larger matters, her respect for her parents bordered on a reverence that is almost impossible to imagine today. They were gods of the household, and lined up behind them were a phalanx of "givens" one didn't challenge or question, such as the existence of God or the lawfulness of racial discrimination, the superiority of man over woman, white over black. It was unusual in that era for a Southern woman to attend a four-year college, much less a Northern one, and it was a prison sentence for this bright and original girl who was both highly competitive and lacking a single academic bone in her body. And it was May Belle's death, not good behavior, that got her off after less than a year.

May Belle had never gotten past high school but spoke French as fluently as English, read widely and subscribed to highbrow journals from Europe as well as American periodicals, had wanted to be a doctor or a scientist. It was these thwarted dreams her daughter was expected to fulfill. In fact, Margaret was out of her element at Smith, unpopular, unsuccessful academically. She did find she could make friends and hold her own among her house-mates by becoming the clown and raconteur. She'd also become engaged: to a fellow from Connecticut named Clifford Henry whom she'd met when he was on leave in Atlanta. He was a shy, sensitive boy, very much in the mold of Ashley. Their romance was entirely by correspondence: in a matter of months, he would sustain a war injury and die. But a saving grace of her time at Smith was an Amherst man named Allen Edee, first a beau, then a friend and correspondent. After a visit to a snobbish aunt in Greenwich, Connecticut, over New Year's, and suffering a hu-miliating experience as a wallflower on New Year's Eve, she sank into a depression, and Edee pulled her out of it. She set out to snare this attractive senior from Nebraska with an arsenal of seductive techniques that would find their way into Scarlett's repertoire. Then, as soon as he fell for her, Margaret began an elaborate push-pull game in which she kept him both near and at bay, playing the ingenue to his Don Juan, rejecting what she called his "bolshevisticly-Byronic" approach to love and anything that smacked of sex, but mothering, teasing, and confiding in him through a correspondence that continued after she returned home. To him she would confide her writing struggles, and Edee would become the recipient of some of her sharpest sketches of the painful and hilarious episodes in her single-girl career.

But at Smith she had to endure not only Clifford Henry's death but, a few months later, her mother's. These two distant people she'd barely known, who died within months of each other and left her bereft, immediately became idealized and eventually conflated into the otherworldly but unreachable characters of *Gone with the Wind*. As a woman dedicated to helping others, the unstintingly noble May Belle Mitchell, like Ellen O'Hara, went out at all hours, but also like Ellen, she neglected home and family. Ellen dies when she contracts the typhoid from the Slatterys, the poor whites she is tending, when Scarlett is nineteen; May Belle died in 1919 from the virus she contracted while out helping others during the flu epidemic. It was the middle of Margaret's first year at Smith.

For her daughter, May Belle's death was both a devastating blow and a strange release. After her death, Margaret was only too glad to have an excuse to come home and tend to her father and brother. It was both an alibi for quitting school and the role she thought her mother would want her to fulfill. "If I can't be first I'd rather be nothing," she once said, which is why her failure to make an impression at Smith caused particular chagrin.

The duty to care for her father and brother had been bequeathed to her, but in an ambiguous manner. In an extraordinary letter written when she knew she was dying, a passionate directive full of mixed messages, May Belle urges her daughter to "give of yourself with both hands and overflowing heart, but give only the excess after you have lived your own life." Then, "This is badly put. What I mean is that your life and energies belong first to yourself, your husband and your children." In one breath she counsels her not to stint on love and attention at home (guilt on her part for her own extracurricular activities?) but with the next immediately cautions her against giving too much when it comes to caring for her widowed father: "never let his or anyone else's life interfere with your real life." A poignant litany of confused priorities and hidden regrets, things not sorted out and perhaps impossible to resolve.

Gerald O'Hara, addled by Ellen's death, was one more burden on his overstrained daughter, and Margaret found that caring for her brother and the uxorious Eugene Mitchell fell far short of a nobly fulfilling vocation, was in fact a thankless and backbreaking task. No wonder her mother had spent so much time away from home. As Margaret eased herself away from the hearth and into the world, we have to wonder (as she no doubt did) what

May Belle would have made of the racy activities of her daughter's generation, now anointed with collective labels—flaming youth, the lost generation—who smoked, drank, kicked up their heels, read Freud, talked dirty, necked in automobiles, blurred social and gender boundaries, all in revolt against what they saw as the narrow-minded strictures of the parents and leaders who had sent their children into an alien war in Europe. May Belle and her feminist allies had taken to the streets, the courts, the legislatures, and their hard work had won women the vote. Now their daughters enjoyed freedoms that weren't quite what the suffragettes had in mind. They went to speakeasies, bobbed their hair, applied makeup, wore short dresses with boyish lines, petted and flirted, and worshipped youth. What would Ellen O'Hara have made of her daughter's transformation into fiancé-stealing, twice-married businesswoman with shady ethics and a life on her hands?

One of the most moving scenes in both book and movie is when Scarlett, hitting the bottle after Frank Kennedy's death, confesses her culpability to Rhett. Her mind turns to her mother, to how disappointed in her daughter she would be. Vivien Leigh's relationship with her own mother had apparently been similarly strained, and she brings an aching poignancy to the scene. Never has she seemed more like a lost child than when she turns from Gable and expresses relief that her mother's dead and can't see her as she is now.

Even more than her contemporaries, Mitchell was fascinated

by psychoanalysis, by Freud, Carl Jung, Alfred Adler, by the new terminology, and espoused at least in theory the principle that the unleashing of one's sexual inhibitions was the royal path to happiness. Margaret had once defied her mother by reading thrillers and romances, and she now debased her mother's memory with an even more scandalous list: Freud, Jung, Adler, and "pornography" such as the works (all banned!) of Frank Harris and Havelock Ellis, John Cleland's *Fanny Hill*, and *Jurgen* (a sort of R-rated *Lord of the Rings*), by Richmond's own James Branch Cabell. Both repulsed and fascinated by sex, she later bragged that she owned more volumes of Havelock Ellis than any other writer, quite a feat, since those massive tomes would strain any library shelf. The pioneering sexologist devoted much attention to frigidity in women and was himself an oddity, a virgin when he married in 1891 at thirty-two (to a lesbian) and impotent until sixty, when he discovered his own particular erotic niche: urolagnia, especially the sight of a woman urinating.

But in "liberated" 1919, there were soldiers to comfort and entertain before they returned to the front, racy books to read, parties to attend. Margaret's brother and friends might be sent abroad. In the meantime, there were nonstop parties for the officers stationed nearby, providing an interlude of breakneck fun. There were fleeting but precious meetings with young men who might go off to fight and die and with whom flirting was virtually one's patriotic duty. Margaret, who'd had traumatic interludes of ostracism and awkwardness, owing perhaps to her unsettled personality, was finding her sea legs, fascinated—if also baffled—by the sudden shift in women's roles.

The war was as much pretext and rationale as cause, as F. Scott Fitzgerald showed when *This Side of Paradise*, his autobiographical first novel, came out in 1920 and alerted a shocked reading public that the wild behavior had been going on before anyone went overseas. Mitchell once called it "the most perfect crystallization of an era in all American fiction." (Part of Mitchell's passionate response to *This Side of Paradise* may have come from identifying with Fitzgerald as an Irish-Catholic outsider among WASPs and a young man with a failure of a father struggling to keep up with the "in" group of Old Guard rich.) Girls, to Fitzgerald's mingled shock, enjoyment, and alarm, had begun taking the initiative, testing the waters, breaching the boundaries of respectability. Rosalind Connage, about to become the love of Amory Blaine's life in *This Side of Paradise*, indulges in typically bad behavior according to her sister, Cecelia: "Smokes sometimes, drinks punch, frequently kissed—Oh, yes—common knowledge—one of the effects of the war, you know." Mobility itself was the most significant factor in the sense of a generation uprooted from its Victorian moorings. Young people courting were no longer confined to the family parlor or subject to the disapproving parental eye, but with this exhilarating freedom came confusion and the loss of an automatic sense of direction. Amory Blaine observes that "the belle had become the flirt, the flirt had become the baby vamp." Where once a kiss meant an engagement, nice girls now "treat men terribly," are "vampires." There's something both brutalizing and liberating in this new indifference to social opinion.

◼

What was girls' role in the newly emancipated social order? How daring could they be and still remain respectable? This burning question for Margaret and her contemporaries she would address, directly or indirectly, in everything she did—in her life, in her writings for the *Atlanta Journal*, and in *Gone with the Wind*. This was particularly urgent for Southern girls, for whom womanhood was virtually synonymous with purity and chastity, the cornerstone of the code of chivalry. Upon her sacred virtue rested the whole self-cleansing apparatus of white male supremacy. The Southern woman was born into a web of self-justifying paradox, a Victorian mix of privileges and penalties that would anchor upper-class values for a very long time. As the pious and self-effacing mistress of the house, she was vested with moral authority. If this gave her no direct power over the affairs of men, it was nevertheless "real," setting her up as a kind of beacon or muse, the example and conscience by which her world was kept pure (Melanie as the true lady whom Rhett reveres). She was strength itself, this "steel magnolia," yet her perceived helplessness and vulnerability provided the raison d'être for the Southern gentleman's code of honor and protection.

The very term "Southern womanhood" is a seductive rhetorical snare, seeming to represent an entire homogenous group while referring to a small, though important (and self-important) elite. As in all preindustrial societies, the upper class gets to create its own mythology because it's the only class that can speak for itself. If the laborers and farmers and frontierspeople, those without education or a political voice, had little to say about the Civil War and the society that came out of it, "Southern womanhood" was no less restricted, a group that excluded not only black women but poor white women as well. The latter, as Victoria Bynum shows in her study of North Carolina's *Unruly Women*, were even more degraded because their position was more shameful. There was no middle-class female culture.

Nor could "Southern womanhood" exist without cavaliers to worship at the foot of the pedestal. A woman of any class without a man was a woman bereft, depersonalized, without guardian or social standing. The planter society might disappear, a middle class gradually emerge. But for the Southern upper-class woman of whom we speak, the necessity for a husband and a place in society hadn't changed at all. From the day of her odyssey on the road to Jonesboro, when her mother exposed her to the spectacle of spinsters and widows, as derelict and abandoned as their homes, Mitchell understood this. An education was indispensable, no less so a husband. At Twelve Oaks, surrounded by men and snubbed by women, Scarlett is referred to by the dread word "fast," a deal-breaker where marriage was concerned. Sometimes Scarlett sounds like Fitzgerald's well-bred and well-kissed Rosalind, who "wants what she wants when she wants it" and "wants people to like her, but if they do not, it never worries or changes her." And like Scarlett, Rosalind detests women. "They represented qualities that she felt and despised in herself—incipient meanness, conceit, cowardice and petty dishonesty." Is Scarlett's contempt for other women an outlet for Margaret Mitchell's revenge on those beastly schoolgirls?

There's a new leeway for women, but the old Victorian conflicts still exist. The Jazz Age, for all its obsession with sex, was more talk than action, since pregnancy without marriage was then and until very recently a fate worse than death. The education of the belle is of a specific sort (Fitzgerald again, of Rosalind): "The education of all beautiful women is the knowledge of men." That wasn't the education May Belle had in mind for her daughter, yet it was, too. In this period of unprecedented freedom and transition, yet bound by old laws and instincts and prejudices, how could you be a belle and a feminist? A belle and a writer? Weren't they mutually exclusive? They were if you were as pretty and gregarious as Margaret, who in the nomenclature version of bobbing your hair had now rechristened herself Peggy. Determined to be popular, the newly minted flapper had chosen a saucy name that had nothing to do with her family.

It was insistence on the cosmic importance of being a lady that Margaret detested in her mother: the emphasis on the surface values of dress, manners, obedience to archaic rules. One of the exhilarating aspects of war, in *Gone with the Wind*, is that, in plunging the world into crisis, it releases women from the confining rules and petty obsessions of everyday life. Scarlett hasn't got time to worry about whether we love her or not; she drops the coquette act, then trots it out occasionally, only to have Rhett or Mammy call her bluff. War justifies her masculinization; crisis allows women to shed ladylike passivity and come into their own as competent agents. Formalities can be skipped, and all those terribly important surface obsessions fall by the wayside.

It was time for Margaret, back in Atlanta and bored and exasperated with taking care of her brother and always critical father, to learn another part, one that would satisfy her mother's standards but also fit more nearly with her own temperament and desires. Why not "come out," find her place in Atlanta society as a debutante? But where *is* her place, where the all-important mother who could sponsor and comfort her? Like Scarlett without Ellen, Margaret lacked the "backing" so important to a young woman but threw herself into the debutante whirl, first almost mockingly, as a dissident and rebel, then posing for her debutante photos in seductive stances and low-cut gowns. Now, in wildly varying roles and costumes captured in the social and gossip columns, she seemed to be casting about like a Hollywood starlet not yet slotted into a type: was she a heavy-lidded sophisticate, a sensualist, a cool number, or a cutie? She'd never found a single style of self-expression. It's as if part of her—the outsider, the skeptic—found the whole debutante gig ridiculous while another, larger part was having a blast, discovering that she could hold her own among the country-club set. She might act out her rebellion against upper-crust society, but she was not about to sacrifice its privileges.

The demon soon got the best of her when she performed the notorious Apache dance that made the gossip columns (no trace of the publicity-shy homebody to come) and shocked the club ladies who made sure she would never be invited to join the Junior League. There were penalties to being unladylike. Yet even as she was making a spectacle of herself that would have appalled her mother, she did penance to May Belle in the socially approved way of volunteer work at a hospital in the black and charity wards.

At the same time, still living with and serving father and brother, she was writing short stories, then tearing them up. Wrestling in particular with one about a writer-heroine, she became blocked and confused about what she could and couldn't express in the voice of this character (it would be a "betrayal" to describe her feelings about a kiss!), leading to a struggle with what she called a "black depression." She had another riding accident in 1920 and was in and out of the hospital with what she described as intestinal adhesions. Numerous ailments followed, and the confusion continued, as she couldn't decide, when she wrote to friends, if she was truly suffering or a psychosomatic mess. She would brag about having the robust constitution of an athlete, "a miniature Dempsey," one minute, and then, with mock-irony, "I'm a fwagile li'l fing." Her biographer Darden Asbury Pyron points out that at this point, before she'd read

Freud and become sensitive to charges of hypochondria, she un-hesitatingly linked her physical ailments with mental problems, admitting that she would "go to pieces under heavy nervous strain." Occasionally she would send Jazz Age stories out to H. L. Mencken, hoping to be published in the *Smart Set* among such notables as Fitzgerald (Mencken had published his first story), Dorothy Parker, Willa Cather, and Ben Hecht. Then, when the manuscripts were returned, she'd be awash in insecu-rity from rejections. Spread thin, wild with energy one minute, subject to anguish and exhaustion the next, at least her foray into the debutante world was beginning to pay off. As a wit, a good-time girl, and (by her own admission) a huge tease, she was grow-ing more confident, surrounded like Scarlett by many of At-lanta's most eligible bachelors.

Being a flirt was the time-honored way of skirting temptation, getting a taste of sex but within the limits of propriety. Peggy-the-tease would encourage men's flattery, then write mortified entries in her journal after petting episodes. To Allen Edee, her friend from Smith days, now her epistolary soul mate, she con-veyed a scathing view of marriage. In one letter, she suggests that the boredom of marriage might be relieved by putting arsenic in the husband's soup. "It's quite a different thing to see a man twice a week on dress parade, when you both sit circumspectly on op-posite sides of a squashy sofa and discuss nails in the barrel indus-try or the price of cheese, *but*—three times a day for three hundred and sixty-five days a year—and just think Al, he might live more than a year!"

Note that in a style given to shortcuts and elisions, she writes out of the number 365 in its full word value, prolonging the sense of a year into dreary infinitum. This was heresy, breathed only by the most daring of Jazz Age ladies. She would have concurred with Gloria Patch, the slightly mad beauty in *The Beautiful and Damned*, who commanded her husband not to call her "wife." "I'm your mistress. Wife's such an ugly word."

Scarlett, smitten by Ashley and no great philosopher, hasn't her creator's corrosive view of the marriage game—at least not yet—but there's plenty of evidence to assist young readers—and viewers of the movie—should they and we be open to such dark and socially suicidal thoughts. At the Twelve Oaks barbecue a Scarlett in full bewitchment mode glances in disgust at the side-lined women, many of them older, some barely older than herself, dowdy in their obligatory matron garb, looking like "a clump of fat crows." She never makes the connection that marriage to Ashley, her dearest wish, would lead to precisely that purdah-like status. Scarlett's not alone in her adolescent blindness. Mitchell understands that, "like most girls, her imagination carried her just as far as the altar and no further."

Yet . . . some of us, like Scarlett and unlike Ellen, "found the road to ladyhood hard," and some of us, straining under the equivalent of an eighteen-inch "bombazine" and other contortions of fifties Southern womanhood, wondered like Scarlett, like Mitchell, why "a girl has to be so silly to catch a husband."

After attending a wedding, Mitchell writes to Edee, in a caustic vein, "There's no thrill comparable to the one that comes only when 'Here comes the Bride' sounds from behind the palms, and the bridal party, heralded by two hysterical infants scattering flowers, comes stalking grimly in. The groom is maudlin with fright and maintains a pretense of composure only by the aid of whispered curses from the best man. Of course, the bride looks beautiful then, if she never looks pretty again, and everybody whispers, 'Isn't she sweet?' Some way they get thru the hectic performance and then everybody kisses the bride, and in the confusion, the best man manages to kiss all the bridesmaids. Everybody wolfs a lot of indigestible grub, and after commenting '*Such* a sweet wedding. What can she see in him?' they go home."

She concludes, "Lord! Weddings are enough to try the most iron nerves! I always weep at weddings—weep from the sheer horror of imagining that it might be mine! There on the 'Altar of Love,' I renew my vows of celibacy." And yet, she soon found herself at that very altar, not once, but twice.

■

Margaret Mitchell was no intellectual and no social revolutionary. Her antics were more for show than substance, she never left Atlanta, never expressed a radical political viewpoint. She never placed herself at odds with her environment as did, say, Lillian Smith, who a decade later staked out a position as a fiery scourge of Southern racism (*Killers of the Dream* and the miscegenation novel *Strange Fruit*) but who also lived, as a lesbian and progressive, outside the little world into which she'd been born. Or Richmond's Ellen Glasgow, who a decade earlier began her own struggle to transcend parochialism while celebrating the Old South's romantic traditions. Or Georgia's own Frances Newman, who actually preceded Mitchell at the *Atlanta Journal* and in two novels (*The Hard-Boiled Virgin* and *Dead Lovers Are Faithful Lovers*) used cryptic language and a convoluted style (the ironic compound negative) to mimic the evasions of Southern society. All three of these women looked to Europe for literary models and found there a context for taking themselves seriously. Mitchell, reacting against her mother's austere syllabus, brandished her vulgar tastes like a weapon of defense, but in taking the low road, deprived herself of a context, a conceptual framework, for taking herself seriously—a difficult thing for a Southern "lady" to do in the best of cases. Society came calling, and she threw in her lot with her genteel compatriots, partied with them, exchanged gossip, attended the ill, and was attended in turn. Yet she wasn't quite of them, either. The furtive writer at home, the social butterfly on the scene, she was walking a tightrope, maintaining, as outsider/insider, a precarious foothold in both worlds and slipping off more and more frequently into illness and pain.

If nothing else, her dim view of marriage put her distinctly at odds with Southern ladyhood's general view of that most sacred calling. But the person who poked such gimlet-eyed fun—"What can she see in him?"—made two very peculiar marriages of precisely the kind that mystified her friends. This petite flirt who could have had her pick of Atlanta's eligibles chose two that were neither. John Robert Marsh, her second husband, was at least respectable, which is more than can be said for Berrien Kinnard Upshaw, nicknamed Red. How could she? asked her family and friends when she gave her hand to Red, a loser with a streak of violence. How can she, they asked again, when she became engaged to Red's roommate, John Marsh, unambitious middle manager in an electric utility company. Red at least had an unsavory reputation that might fire the imagination. He was a sometime bootlegger, a rogue in the manner of, but nowhere near as attractive as, Rhett Butler. He was unstable, unpopular, and impecunious, but he had two things that apparently spoke to her—a mysterious sexual charge and a need to be mothered. Marsh, the former newspaperman, was sober, conservative, something of a milquetoast, and an unlikely person to share digs with the flamboyant Red except as an attraction of opposites. It gets stranger: John served as best man for the wedding of the woman who a few years later would be his bride, and the groomsmen were all former beaux of Margaret's. The Episcopal ceremony was Margaret's final break with Catholicism, even with organized religion, and the beginning of the end of her relationship with her grandmother Stephens. (Perhaps "God did not frighten her anymore.")

But it's possible to see these two marriages, in retrospect, as having served extraordinary ulterior purposes. If marrying Red Upshaw was a way to escape the boiling pot of horrors of the Mitchell household, she landed in a domestic fire of a different kind . . . and, because the newlyweds were so poor, living in that same household. Red was no breadwinner, and they were soon so mired in debt that she had to take a job. In other words, she had an airtight alibi for doing what she secretly wanted to do anyway. She applied for a job on the *Atlanta Journal*. Nice girls, especially nice married girls, didn't work. It was poaching on male territory, it reflected badly on one's husband. Only a compelling reason like impending poverty would justify such a radical step. So few women worked at the time, especially in the South, and more especially in "society," and newspapers were a man's world. On the other hand, it was an accredited paying job, like any other; it didn't demand the risk, self-exposure, and arrogance of setting oneself up as a fiction writer.

She decided on John's advice to skip the city room and apply to Angus Perkerson, the editor of the *Atlanta Journal*'s Sunday features magazine and no great fan of women employees. He turned her over to his coeditor and wife, Medora, both of them expecting that, if she showed up, she'd do a few frothy pieces on the debutante scene. Instead, she arrived early, worked like a demon, and gravitated to stories that weren't social notes but sociological forays. From 1922 to 1926, when the painful ankle injury forced her to retire, she did everything from proofreading and book reviewing to writing gossip and personality sketches. She interviewed visiting dignitaries (there were pieces on Rudolph Valentino and Teddy Roosevelt) and did a series of inside stories on the federal prison in Atlanta, but her specialty became short articles on contemporary trends and topics told in her own inimitable mixture of acerbic forthrightness and demure femininity. She would take hold of an incident or a person or a trend and turn it into an issue—the flapper phenomenon, for example, its charms and excesses. A funny piece on the dangers of Valentino's "Argentine Tango," as practiced by slower-moving Southern damsels tripping over themselves and their partners. Articles on fashions in dress, slang, lipstick (an "Anti-Lipstick Crusade"— how much is too much makeup? Chewing gum, yes or no?).

But sexual manners and mores underlay even the lightest of these articles, the topic she returned to again and again. "Jobs before Marriage for High School Girls" polls a graduating class and finds the majority most interested in acceptably feminine jobs in "social service," "teaching," and "working with people," but a few express dangerous ambitions to be reporters, actresses, and surgeons. And "Do Working Girls Make the Best Wives?" and if so why? If there's choice, when is it fashionable for a woman to work, and for how long? The consensus is "Not after children." Her descriptions of young women behaving outrageously, chewing gum at weddings and funerals, and dissing their elders, of the gap between the generations, bear a superficial resemblance to the wild young things who shock their elders in Evelyn Waugh's postwar London or Fitzgerald's Northeast, but without the grasp of history or wider frame of reference. Young people exhibiting bad manners but refusing to settle for the pieties and arrangements of their elders are their mutual subject, but Mitchell's pieces were very much of their period and genre: uneven, girlish, and ephemeral, with that dashed-off air that was part of the generation's cultivated attitude of indifference but is also what prevents us from taking her and her subjects seriously. Her vignettes do show her excellent ear for dialogue and gift for characterization, and in some, those dealing with unusual or intelligent women, her voice seems to take on a tone of maturity, as if she herself were rising to meet their challenge. With the young subjects of her pieces, she is noncommittal, and you can see why Mencken turned down her Jazz Age stories: there is no original voice, and the tone is facetious rather than genuinely sharp or satirical. Unlike Anita Loos or Dorothy Parker, she is unable to play the faux-naïf or take the moral high ground. Like Fitzgerald, she's highly ambivalent toward these ill-mannered nineteen- and twenty-year-old exhibitionists and the incivility and immorality that seem a necessary part of their new freedoms. Unlike Fitzgerald, however, she doesn't know how to write herself through or out of this ambivalence.

Where Mitchell suddenly acquires a point of view and a firmer tone, a real orientation, is when she begins to interview and write about older women. Not the generation of her parents but that of her grandparents, the women who'd lived through the Civil War. In a series she writes on "romantic couples" she's most excited by Fanny Kemble, the British actress and abolitionist memoirist who married the wealthy slave-owning Georgia planter Pierce Butler. Kemble influenced Britain's decision not to side with the South in the Civil War, and her scathing memoir, writes Mitchell, "had more influence in arousing anti-slavery sentiments than any other book published at the time."

Suffrage goes unmentioned—having the vote seems not to have interested her in the least—but she was an instinctual feminist, constantly gravitating to strong women. Just after the "romantic couples," she wrote her breakout articles, all under her new nom de plume, Peggy Mitchell (not only changing her first name but retaining her maiden name, inescapably an affront to the husband at home). At the library she dug up the stories of four remarkable women of Georgia, a project that allowed her to taste with growing confidence the pleasures of historical research while nourishing her fascination with strong women. Like the females in her childhood plays, they were Amazonians, trespassing on male turf while nevertheless "carrying on the [pioneer] tradition of Georgia's noble womanhood."

Rebecca Latimer Felton, married to a U.S. congressman, read omnivorously on affairs of the world, made speeches, and participated fully in her husband's political campaigns. When another

Georgia senator, Tom Watson, died, the governor appointed her to fill his place, and she went to Washington in 1922 to become the first female U.S. senator.

"Cross-eyed Nancy Hart," six feet tall, a famous cook, was fearless but with no sweetness in her personality. (Nor was any necessary, Mitchell emphasizes: it was during the Revolution, when homes were subjected to marauding Whigs and Tories.) The enemy landed on her doorstep and invaded her kitchen. Husband and family fled, but the ferocious homemaker pulled out a rifle and singlehandedly captured the six Tories who tried to eat her pumpkin pie.

"Private Bill, Soldierette," tells of the valiant fighter known as Private Bill Thompson. Not until her "buddy" was killed in the Second Battle of Bull Run was Bill revealed as a woman and her buddy's wife. Lucy Mathilda Kenny of Savannah had enlisted with her husband at the outbreak of war and had fought in numerous battles at his side.

Mary Musgrove, a young Indian woman who spoke both Creek and English, was an intermediary between the colonists and the Creek. At the instigation of her third husband, the penniless Reverend Bosomworth, however, she declared herself empress of the Creek Nation and led her tribe on the warpath. They demanded that the colonists return formerly held Indian land. Governor Oglethorpe eventually outsmarted them, but Mary survived, "an untamed savage until she died."

She would seek out especially the old ladies of the Confederacy, conducting endless interviews, asking lifestyle questions that weren't on the agenda, gleaning material that would authenticate details of the antebellum social scene. Her imagination was seeking its natural home, the world of the stories she'd been born into on her grandmother's porch, the characters she'd heard about from relatives and pictured in those mansions on the Jonesboro Road.

One of the most intriguing interviews is with Mrs. William Baker, best friend and, at eighty-seven, the last remaining bridesmaid to Mittie Bullock Roosevelt, Theodore's Southern mother. Baker's white-columned colonial was right in the middle of red-clay Tara country, as was Bullock Hall. Surely some of this grandeur seeps into the portrait, if not of Tara, then of Twelve Oaks and the preposterously lavish, slave-sustained entertaining. Baker recalls the wedding of 1853, a days-long affair, when ice was brought in from Savannah to make ice cream. Yet there were economies to be made: according to David McCullough in his Roosevelt family biography, *Mornings on Horseback*, four slaves had to be sold to pay for the wedding.

Then, ten months after they tied the knot, the hopeless Upshaw marriage unraveled. For a moment, Margaret spread her wings. She took off, alone, for Latin America of all places, and arrived in Cuba, where she found herself lonely, isolated, and menaced in a culture unused to the sight of a single woman tourist. She took from this distressing episode an odd lesson, but one she was apparently ready to hear: the terrible vulnerability of the unmarried woman. The trip to Cuba put an abortive end to her wanderlust and led to the next step, a second marriage, but of a different kind. She would settle down into cozy domesticity with a "safe" man—John—with a "regular" job.

The union with Red had crashed around her in a horrifying way. Increasingly enraged and jealous—of her work, of former rivals—Red beat her on at least two occasions. They were still living with Margaret's family, penniless and fighting constantly. Then he went crazy. First he walked out, raising in her the age-old fear of abandonment, but to it was added guilt: had she provoked the departure, the indifference? It was unbearable though finally preferable to what followed: episodes of such violence that she wound up in court, filing for divorce, with bruises all over her body and an injured eye providing sufficient cause. There were hints of rape or attempted rape, then and later, when he barged in one day after her marriage to John and charged upstairs, where she was dressing. They were interrupted by the housekeeper, but whatever he did, it had none of the cathartic effect of the scene it inspired in the book and movie. The event prompted endless musings and even self-recriminations in her journal, as she continued to wonder if and to what extent she had provoked the attack. Meanwhile, still in terror that he would return (she knew she had a sneaking attraction to the threat of caveman violence), she kept a pistol in her bedside table.

Rejecting the role of victim, she turned to the dependable if boring John—the "slug," as some of her friends called him—

more Frank Kennedy than Ashley. Yet, comically, the slug had feet as cold as hers when they decided to take the plunge. The man who had written long letters to his mother extolling the "liberal platonism" he and Margaret had enjoyed in their courtship now wrote of the impending nuptials in singularly unecstatic terms: "We have decided to toss our several distastes for matrimony into the lake, and give the ancient and honorable institution a try."

Hardly had he won the reluctant permission of Margaret's father when he fell ill with what Margaret described as "Flu— a brand new type, the 'hiccoughing flu.'" This strange onset lasted . . . and lasted. After three weeks of John's nonstop hiccuping, she checked him into a hospital so that she could continue working. There were seizures and other odd and puzzling symptoms, but Margaret, despite her vaunted psychoanalytic keenness, furiously rejected any diagnosis that hinted of a neurotic or psychosomatic interpretation, even as the two of them fell over each other to see who could get sick next. With John, there had been and would be endless bouts of illness—scarlet fever, dyspepsia, and other digestive problems, many residual from his time in the army. When he was finally released from the hospital, he was still weak and sick, with huge medical bills, but she rushed to play nurse, a role that made her feel useful and seemed to incline her— indeed both of them—into hastening the marriage rather than otherwise. His protectiveness of her matched her desire to "serve" him, and this series of alternating his-and-her illnesses and infirmities presumably removed sex from the table, and the roles of mutual nurturing provided a deeply comforting substitution.

■

The sardonic disparager of marriage would become, to all the world, a devoted housewife, but for a man who was an authority figure in name only, a sort of surrogate mother who, having little ego of his own and little in the way of career, could turn his full attention to her. The "liberal platonist" (no Byronic Marxist he) would make no great demands in the bedroom, which was fine since the sex-averse Margaret had an even greater horror of pregnancy and childbirth. She made no secret of her distaste for children, both real-life ones and those she came upon, too frequently, in novels. She shuddered comically at ill-behaved tots and in true agony at stories of stillbirths and abortions. She was too private to go into her own negative feelings but claimed poverty, huge debts, fear of illness, and further debts as possible alibis in what would be seen as the Marshes' failure to produce offspring.

As vice president of publicity for the Georgia Power and Light Company, John was making enough money that they could move out of their first apartment, called affectionately but without apparent exaggeration "the Dump," into a slightly larger apartment. But in her letters there was suddenly a constant flow of symptoms, both hers and John's (she even reported malaria at one point). And it was exactly nine months after her wedding that she first mentioned an ankle problem. No one remembered having heard of the ankle before, but suddenly it was so incapacitating she could barely walk, and then only with a brace and the horrible orthopedic shoes, signifying the rheumatic arthritis that had now become her life companion. In the curious symbiosis that was becoming the unspoken contract of their marriage, illness and self-proclaimed poverty made it possible to no longer think seriously about having children. John had suffered seizures at one point, and the fear of epilepsy became a plausible reason for the Marshes to forgo procreation. Sexual abstinence would create its own substitutes. The two of them in effect became their own children, taking their daily temperature, worrying bravely for public consumption.

Though she and John still entertained and saw people in a slapdash fashion, their illnesses kept them sidelined for long periods. Peggy had become, in the words of Virginia Woolf's essay "On Being Ill," a "deserter" from the "army of the upright." She had "dropped out of the race" and was therefore exempt from the "genial pretense" that healthy people must maintain, the responsibility for oiling the social wheels that falls especially on women. For the sick there is pain, weariness, and discomfort, but there is also an exhilarating dispensation—room for the imagination to roam, for energy to be redirected.

Barren and infertile, at least by the customs of the country, the Marsh union would incubate a giant offspring known as *Gone with the Wind.* Now, with her ankle in traction, Margaret was unable to work, so John (ambulatory for the time being) brought her stacks of books from the public library, Civil War history because she'd gone through most of the novels. With John and her books, she had finally found the person and the context for taking her writing seriously, if only in secret. It was as if her husband were planting the seed for the project that would bring them closer. He encouraged her when she began writing her novel, became her editor and cheerleader, prod and scourge, the without-which-not of *Gone with the Wind.*

In misery herself, she wrote the bleak last chapter, Melanie's death, Rhett's renunciation, Scarlett's final obtuseness. "She never understood either of the men she loved and so she lost them both." Had Margaret ever understood the opaque, asexual Clifford Henry? Or the mad and unstable Red Upshaw? Encouraged by John's enthusiasm, she went back to the beginning, proceeding on an old typewriter in a corner of the apartment, and put on green eyeshades and pants to feel more like a reporter. She was writing—a lady always needed an excuse, a cover—*because* of her physical disability. Still, since she was no longer a reporter with a job, her identity was now ambiguous, her work, known only by hints and gossip, the scribblings of a dilettante. She was hugely ambitious but had to pretend otherwise, even to herself. To those who knew or suspected her activity, she was, in the words of another biographer, Anne Edwards, "a housewife with a hobby." What did she do to justify her existence? She wrote a book. What did she do to justify writing a book? She said it was just for the enjoyment of herself and her husband, that she had no intentions of publishing. And indeed, the secret shroud in which she wrapped the project in part supports that claim. Secrecy, and keeping it within the family, had other motives, too. She genuinely feared she could never publish the book because people she knew would see themselves in the characters—particularly her grandmother and Red Upshaw—and perhaps sue.

She was, moreover, beset by paralyzing feelings of inadequacy. John brought her books by F. Scott Fitzgerald and Ellen Glasgow, and she was in awe. In comparison with them, she knew she'd never be a prose stylist. After reading Stephen Vincent Benet's famous epic poem about the Civil War, *John Brown's Body*, which appeared in 1928, she stopped writing for three months. How could she presume to write about the Civil War after that? Yet she kept on . . . and on. This perseverance alone gives the lie to her assertion that she never meant to publish, as do other facts, such as her painstaking research, her appeals to and reliance on John for lengthy and numerous editing suggestions, and her native ambition: a desire to prove herself, and especially to *disprove* her father's dim view of her writing abilities.

If the mother had been a harsh taskmaster, the father went beyond that into a pathological mean-spiritedness. Eugene Mitchell, a prig and a snob who fancied himself a serious historical scholar, widowed and dyspeptic, hadn't thought much of his daughter's journalism and now said aloud that he didn't expect she could be writing anything worth reading. Astonishingly—or maybe not—after the book appeared, his response was not just withholding but downright nasty. To a friend's query as to whether he'd reread *Gone with the Wind*, he replied that "nothing in the world would induce him to read the book again and that nothing in the world except that [Peggy] was his child induced him to read it originally."

Anxieties and interruptions, including the usual catalog of Southern Lady social obligations—friends' weddings, illnesses, funerals—along with Marsh malingerings, kept her writing, and not writing, and then, after more or less finishing the manuscript in 1930, correcting, revising, and hesitating to let it go. It lay in its manila envelopes, one for each chapter, stashed everywhere in the apartment, until the vacillations that led to its surrender, practically a slapstick comedy routine, a tug-of-war with the publishing world on one end of the rope and Margaret on the other, clutching her tattered manuscript, refusing to let go.

In 1935, Harold Latham of Macmillan had been given Margaret's name by Lois Cole, who'd become a friend of hers while heading up Macmillan's Georgia branch. Cole knew about the secret project and had firsthand experience of her friend's vivid storytelling powers. There was a fancy luncheon for Georgia writers that Margaret was just barely able to attend: a few months before, while the Marshes were driving in their recently acquired automobile (their first), there had been a terrible accident. Peggy had been at the wheel, suffered a snapped neck, and was bedridden for three months suffering from pain and nausea. She and

Latham were seated together at the luncheon, but when he asked her about the reported novel, she insisted there was no such thing. She continued her denials while driving him around Atlanta, showing him the sights and discussing Southern writers.

Bone tired, she nevertheless fulfilled her commitment to escort other writers home from the conference. But part of the fatigue was more than the residual pain from the accident: it was exasperation from listening all day while writers with less talent than she had were praised as Georgia's future literary lions. This and her father's dismissive attitude finally persuaded her to give up the manuscript. In the future telling of the story, this chafing of her pride and her sense of psychological injury at the hands of unnamed young women who laughed at the idea that Peggy Mitchell could write a book convinced her to expose her work. Girls laughing at her—it had happened before. Their mocking dismissal now gave her the alibi to commit a nakedly self-promoting act. She had to vindicate herself in the eyes of those who would not take her seriously, eyes that possibly included May Belle's as well.

Impulsively, she called Latham in his hotel room and met him in the lobby, where she sat surrounded by dozens of brown envelopes. Latham took them with him on the train north, reading the murky, scribbled-over typescript the whole way, only to receive a telegram from the anxious author demanding it back! John agreed—it was a mess, with chapters (including the first) missing, repetitions, some of it in illegible scrawl, no title page with author's credit. Latham, already enthusiastic, persuaded her to let him finish reading it. She did, though not without dispatching a lengthy letter enumerating all its faults and omissions. At last a contract was signed. There was much work to be done, including changing the name of Pansy O'Hara to Scarlett and finding a title, but Latham and Macmillan knew they had a hit on their hands.

In the back and forth, there were arguments over Frank Kennedy's death by KKK misadventure (Peggy wanted to eliminate the Klan altogether) and the ending. While readers like Latham appreciated the novel's "irresistible" storytelling momentum but agreed it was no great shakes as literature, no one seems to have grasped how unusual it was to create a heroine of such wicked proportions and treat her in such a nonjudgmental fashion, and to refuse the consolations of a romantic ending. Or rather, they sensed and were leery of its unusualness. Macmillan called on Professor Charles Everett of Columbia as an early reader. His evaluation had been highly enthusiastic but included several objections that Mitchell had mostly addressed. He noted a few, remarkably few, historical inaccuracies—it was he who criticized the KKK episode as written. Everett's most specific objection, however, was to the ending. He was let down by the finality of Rhett's refusal to stay with Scarlett and suggested that Mitchell hint that "she gets him in the end." Margaret's response is a little gem of pseudo-accommodating evasion. She begins by saying that her intention (if she remembers correctly, since "it's been a long time since I even looked at it") was to leave the ending open. But "my idea was that, through several million chapters, the reader will have learned that both Pansy and Rhett are tough characters, both accustomed to having their own way. And at the last, both are determined to have their own ways and those ways are very far apart. And the reader can either decide that she got him or she didn't." The reader can have whatever fantasies he or she wants, but her view of the matter is pretty clear: two obstinate antagonists whose separation is inevitable. Then, with ingratiating deference, she tells Everett and the publisher, "If you don't like the way it looks when you get the final copy, tell me so and I'll change it," which is followed immediately by the adamant "I'll change it any way you want, except to make a happy ending." Her biographer Pyron believes that she did in fact alter the book, which originally ended with Rhett's departure and "My dear, I don't give a damn." He feels that this vivid sentence was meant as conclusion and that the coda—the page and a half after the asterisks—weakens the drama and—more important in his view—undermines the impression that Scarlett has grown and evolved, "changed positively in the ultimate crisis." But this is precisely what's singular and uncompromising about Mitchell's vision: there is no eleventh-hour epiphany, none of that conventional change of heart so beloved of second-rate dramaturgy. Scarlett, unchanged and unchanging, lives in an eternal present. Remorse and regret, anything connected to the past, is emotional baggage that must be shrugged off, as she invokes the denial that allows her to forge ahead.

■

From the date of signing the contract, itself fraught with worries and second-guessing from the "experts" in the Mitchell family, the problems went hand in hand with the delights, both extreme. Under the strain of editing the book (where John's help was crucial) Mitchell developed such severe eyestrain that she was again bedridden, unable even to read or write letters. With the publication of the book, all hell broke loose, and Mitchell's life imploded overnight. John sent a famous telegram to *Time* magazine (which had requested an interview): "MRS MARSH SICK IN BED AS RESULT OF STRAIN OF BECOMING TOO FAMOUS SUDDENLY."

Peggy had to establish rules: no public appearances (unlike May Belle, she was terrified of speaking in public), no autographs, no comments (though this law she occasionally broke for the Georgia papers). And then began the Letters. By a slight stretch of the genre, these would be categorized as thank-you notes, her own lively variations on a certain ritualistic form: first, the long-winded *apology* for lateness, the inadequacy of the letter, and its length (an imposition on the recipient); then *gratitude* and/or compliments, further apologies for her "greenness" at the business of writing (is it appropriate to write and thank a critic?); and finally, her shock, awe, and misery at the phenomenon of the book's success. Published in 1976 as *Margaret Mitchell's "Gone with the Wind" Letters, 1936–1949*, these are unfortunately only a small selection, most having been destroyed by John and Stephens according to her wishes. Caution and diplomacy now governed her life. She knew she was famous and couldn't bear the scrutiny that such fame would bring. Suspecting that someone would one day want to publish her letters, she made sure the most caustic and revealing would be eliminated while checking any outrageous impulses in the ones she did let through. And . . . she was a different woman now.

The flapper had become the matron, the exhibitionist, the recluse. The baby-faced vamp of the teens and early twenties who had scandalized "le tout Atlanta" at a debutante ball had, in an about-face, hung up her dancing shoes and become a secret writer. Her bad ankles now necessitated orthopedic shoes, she drank and ate, had become sedentary and wifely—a "lady" of sorts. But Scarlett wasn't dead, just engaged in long-distance seduction. The flirt was channeled into epistolary form. In 1938 she wrote to Herschel Brickell of the *New York Post* that she had gained weight and had to "unzip all my dresses to breathe. . . . I am as hefty as a hog at killing time." Brickell was among the many who had reviewed the book favorably and been charmed into becoming a regular correspondent and friend. (So intense was their relationship that Peggy was considered one of the reasons for the breakup of his marriage some years later.)

In a thank-you letter to Donald Adams of the *New York Times*

In the opening scene, Scarlett bewitches the Tarleton twins and learns
of Ashley's engagement. *Credit: MGM/Photofest.*

Ashley introduces Melanie to Scarlett at the Twelve Oaks barbecue.
Credit: MGM/Photofest.

Worn by Carol Burnett in the instantly recognizable parody.
Credit: CBS/Photofest.

The memorable green velvet curtain dress, worn by Scarlett to seduce Rhett into paying the tax bill for Tara. *Credit: MGM/Photofest.*

Margaret Mitchell as a nineteen-year-old debutante.
Courtesy of the Kenan Research Center at the Atlanta History Center.

Margaret Mitchell as thirty-five-year-old author, correcting the
manuscript of *Gone with the Wind*. Credit: *Photofest.*

At the bazaar for the Confederacy, Melanie, Scarlett, and Rhett offer up rings for the Noble Cause. *Credit: MGM/Photofest.*

Rhett and Scarlett flee a burning Atlanta and "watch the old South disappear." *Credit: MGM/Photofest.*

William Cameron Menzies's storyboard for the escape from Atlanta.
Credit: Photofest.

David Selznick, Victor Fleming, Vivien Leigh, and Clark Gable
relax on the set. *Credit: Photofest.*

Melanie comforts a tormented Rhett after Scarlett's miscarriage.
Credit: MGM/Photofest.

A drunken Rhett tries to squeeze Ashley out of Scarlett's skull.
Credit: MGM/Photofest.

In the woodshed, Ashley complains to Scarlett about a world "worse than death." *Credit: MGM/Photofest.*

After Bonnie's birth, Mammy finally warms up to Rhett. *Credit: MGM/Photofest.*

Scarlett stretches, smiles, and hums in postcoital delight.
Credit: MGM/Photofest.

Book Review there came a long discussion of Uncle Remus and black dialect. She agrees with his assertion that Uncle Remus wouldn't like it, saying she "sweated blood" (a favorite expression of hers) to keep it from being like Uncle Remus, but that as it happened "his son" (that is, the son of the author Joel Chandler Harris) gave her a rave, his daughter-in-law had written laudatory letters, the granddaughter had written so often in her column as to embarrass Mitchell, and even the grandson "has been one of my kindest press agents." To his expressed hope that she wouldn't set about a second book too soon, she replied in no uncertain terms. "I not only do not intend to set about a book too soon but, thank God, never intend to write another one if I keep my sanity." She explains the hell of the writing as an endless series of deaths, illnesses "in the family and among friends which lasted months and even years, childbirths (not my own!), divorces and neuroses among friends, my own ill health, and four fine auto accidents which did everything from fracturing my skull to splintering my vertebrae." She would no sooner sit down to write than "somebody I loved would decide to have their gall bladder removed or would venture into the office of a psychiatrist and for months thereafter wonder, at the top of their lungs, if they were really realizing their fullest potentialities."

The image is that of a Southern lady whose scribbles are interrupted by all the conventional distractions one would expect of an everyday, homey woman; the neuroses are pointedly those of the proverbial "friends," not herself, of whom no mention of the writerly angst and insecurity that occasionally blocked and paralyzed her. After the book's publication and success and through the long noisy production of the film, letter writing became a full-time occupation, letters the second book she would never write. These garrulous but carefully crafted and flattering missives (her correspondents are always right) amounted to a delicious twist on the old joke about why Southern girls don't go to orgies . . . too many thank-you notes to write. In the Mitchell version, too many thank-you notes is why Southern women don't write best sellers. In any case, she kept the vow that she would never write another novel, and these became the extension of book writing by other means. They put forward a portrait of the lady writer in distress: funny and fairly candid (given the fact that she suspected the letters would be published and so was more restrained and discreet than she was in person) but always ruefully modest, self-effacing, and humorous, unpretentious, and above all, not only unspoiled by success but detesting every minute of it. She bristled at attacks but pretended otherwise, placing her defense in the mouths of others. She wouldn't have written the book, she wrote defensively, if she had cared about the critics, "for the Civil War was deader than Hector and long Victorian novels completely out of style."

In a letter to a Mr. Mark Allen Patton, who, like other of her friends, compared her poor book to *War and Peace*, "saying of course that it didn't approach it but was the nearest thing to it they could think of," she confesses with horror that she will now have to read Tolstoy's novel. She had tried repeatedly but failed to read him and his Russian colleagues, whom she accuses of a "youthful delight in the sordid" and of muddled-headed confused thinking, while confessing to some muddle of her own. Then comes the sore point: "I know I was going to be hammered for my lack of style and I was but it didn't hurt a bit." Then rises up the father in her defense (and apparently something of a fan after all): "he is a lawyer of the careful, cautious old-fashioned kind. He's a Phi Beta Kappa and the most brilliant man I'll ever know. And he shouted, 'What do you mean, "undistinguished style"? Good heavens, I can actually understand every word you write without having to read it twice! In this day and time, that amounts to sheer genius!'"

Her especial gratitude to letter-writers who praised Melanie was perhaps a hunger for approval of the sensible-shoes person she'd grown into by the time she started the book, while her puzzled and disinterested reaction to various views of Scarlett was a confirmation of the degree to which she'd distanced herself from the scapegrace flapper she'd left behind. There was thus an eerie detachment in her enthusiastic response to clinical interpretations of Scarlett's "pathology" from doctors and psychiatrists. The psychoanalyst without portfolio who had told people (possibly to impress her mother and, later, placate her mother's spirit) that she had wanted to go to medical school and become a neurologist or a psychiatrist was delighted at a letter from Dr. Hervey Cleckley. An Atlanta psychiatrist who would afterward write *The Three Faces of Eve*, he had included Scarlett among the fictional case studies in his 1938 book, *The Mask of Sanity*. Mitchell completely agreed that Scarlett fitted into the good doctor's category of those "emotionally impoverished" people he labeled "partial psychopaths," whose "egocentricity is basic" and whose "incapacity for true commitment in love is apparently unmodifiable. . . . Unlike the complete psychopath, she successfully pursues ends that lead to her material being . . . inward hollowness and serious lack of insight."

In another letter, however, to Professor Edwin Granberry of Rollins College, Mitchell expresses gratitude for his kind words about Scarlett and confesses how surprised she was "that such a storm of hard words would descend upon the poor creature's head. She just seemed to me to be a normal person . . . doing the best she could."

■

Normal or a psychopath? Praise or despise? Take your pick. Mitchell was indifferent. Margaret/Peggy wanted to be like Melanie, as Scarlett wanted to be like Ellen, or wanted to *want* to be like Ellen. But Scarlett, like Margaret Mitchell, couldn't help being Scarlett, stuck in her own fierce, desperate, narcissistic adolescence, giving it a voice we all recognize—clever, charming, defiantly philistinish. Scarlett, radical yet recognizable, came from some disavowed part of Mitchell merged with the virago Annie Stephens, the wild girl subdued, now overwhelmed.

Having never graduated to adulthood, she was caught unprepared for the thing May Belle had warned her about on the road to Jonesboro. *Gone with the Wind*, book-movie-phenomenon, was her Civil War, her First World War, and her Great Depression, the thing that turned her life upside down, and she was far from knowing how to deal with it.

The premiere, on December 15, had been planned for months, almost longer than the shooting of the movie. Earlier and for a brief moment, Selznick decided he didn't want the premiere to take place in Atlanta, but the producer was no match for a Southern city scorned. A battalion of matrons descended like Furies on the mayor's office, which in turn issued a proclamation ("the movie belongs to all of us," accent on *us*) demanding that the premiere take place in Atlanta. If the South had lost the war, here was a battle Southerners could win. The world premiere would be their true Redemption. There would be costumes and cocktail parties and lunches, marches by veterans, and the Junior League ball the night before, and every bit as splashy as the premiere itself. Everyone flew down—everyone except Hattie McDaniel and the other blacks in the cast, whose presence in segregated Atlanta was not wanted. In attendance were the Selznickers, Gable with Lombard, Leigh with Olivier, all wreathed in smiles through parades, speeches, banquets. Mitchell had gone into hiding before the great day, skipped the ball in a tasty act of vengeance, but emerged on the fifteenth to attend a press luncheon, where she met Leigh, Gable, and Selznick. Though she hated these occasions, she and John attended the black-tie event, watched while the audience sat rapt, cheered, wept, and finally burst into an ovation. John, in the second of his famous witticisms, remarked after seeing the shot of fallen Confederates: "If we'd had that many soldiers we'd have won the war." And Margaret, inconspicuous in stature and dress and terrified as a public speaker, allowed Gable to escort her to the microphone, where she graciously thanked one and all, from the taxi drivers and librarians to Selznick and the cast. In photographs of the event, she looks like a librarian herself alongside the dazzling Hollywood stars, but she smiles gallantly and no doubt with relief. The movie has been an unqualified success. And however unstarlike a figure Peggy Mitchell cut, she is a hero to her hometown. Atlanta has been vindicated, Sherman's depredations partly avenged.

What had been a steady stream of requests and harassments before the film became a perfect storm after. Now, what with illnesses (hers and John's) and anxiety (hers), she grew more dependent on John to maintain her in her housewifely role. Her housekeeper, Bessie, with whom she was extraordinarily close, was a churchgoing woman of the old school who believed in a wife's subservience to her husband. This attitude plus Peggy's own reliance on John, and her unease about that reliance, made her increasingly shy of the public.

The fanfare that surrounded the book's publication, and then the turmoil over the movie, brought demands and issues that were continuous and overwhelming, There were accusations, for example, that John had helped her write the book, a devastating charge she denied publicly and vehemently. There was the fear of exposure—the Red Upshaw marriage and its aftermath. John had suffered several attacks of epilepsy during the editing, and her guilt toward him drove her further into insisting on his primary role as breadwinner. She had already embraced her dependency on John as an editor—something that bothered her friend Medora Perkerson a lot. Medora, who had so appreciated Peggy's journalistic and storytelling gifts and supported her from the start, was down on John and the marriage, thinking her friend had given up her independence and holding John responsible.

Yet who can judge? If Margaret Mitchell withheld final judgment on the beautiful virago she'd launched on the world with her husband's crucial support; if she left Scarlett's pluses and minuses untotaled and unreconciled, why should we need to pass judgment on a marriage even more ambiguous in its ultimate meaning? Who can unravel the good and bad in such a complex and half-hidden arrangement, which, we can reasonably assume, was the container without which Peggy Mitchell's divided personality would fly apart?

The other vessel for her colliding parts, and for her heroine's, was of course, Atlanta itself, the city, with its headlong rush, its ability to rise quickly from the ashes of war, its crazy mix of old and new. Atlanta might provide a gracious cover for Melanie, but its soul was Scarlett, as greedy as any Yankee carpetbagger, cunning, rapacious, brave, at one with the nouveau capital of the industrial South. Mitchell could never leave it, yet life became increasingly unbearable after the whirlwind years of *Gone with the Wind*. However she might have hated the publicity, the noise, and the lack of privacy, she couldn't quite settle for obscurity either.

Scarlett, clamoring to be the center of attention, would always prevail over modest Melanie. The movie, with its successive revivals, would boost the book and vice versa. Mitchell would emerge for intense activity during the war effort in the forties, and there was endless paperwork over foreign rights, copyright cases, and contractual disputes. With her inherited grasp of the intricacies of copyright she filed a lawsuit over unlawful foreign publications of *Gone with the Wind*. Putting pressure on the appropriate congressman, she instigated a landmark case on foreign rights that would end up protecting American writers. Then there were the minutiae she would obsess over, scouring the press for lies or slurs or simply insignificant errors that would occasion angry letters and demands for apology. These were, presumably, the manic "relief" from depressions and illnesses and increasing isolation.

Thanks to all the barriers she erected to protect her privacy, friends simply stopped dropping in. Then, after John suffered a severe heart attack in 1945 and became a semi-invalid, she seemed to let herself go. She ate and drank too much, gained weight, saw only a few chosen friends, and aged dramatically. To everyone's alarm, she began talking ominously of not having much time left, even told one correspondent that she knew she would die in a car accident. Indeed the old specter of death-by-automobile finally got her: on an August evening in 1949, she persuaded John to take her to the movies. They were crossing Peachtree Street to see the Powell-Pressburger film *A Canterbury Tale* and were in the middle when a car came careening around a corner toward them. John stood still as Margaret, overweight and slowed by her bad ankle, plunged into the road and was hit by the speeding taxi. She died in a hospital five days later without ever recovering consciousness.

FOUR

E Pluribus Unum

The opening scene, when Scarlett bewitches the audience and the Tarleton twins on the veranda of Tara, was, after the burning of Atlanta, the first scene shot. That was on January 26, 1939. And at the end of August, it was also the last. Cukor's initial take had to be scrapped because in Technicolor the hair of the twins (played by Fred Crane and the future Superman, George Reeves) came out a lurid orange, a hue suitable for flames and sunsets but not the hair of men or even simpering swains of the Tarleton type. The twins' curly carrot-top coifs were promptly darkened and slickened, but despite several retakes, Selznick still wasn't pleased. He left it until the end of shooting in June, by which time the exhausted and overworked Leigh looked too old and tired. On July 1 the production folded, everyone left, then after a period of rest for Leigh and the rejuvenating effects of the longed-for reunion with Olivier, she returned for a successful final take, her character as fresh as a newly sprung daisy. Selznick decided a change of costume would enhance her innocence: all white instead of the original green-ruffled dress, the daringly low-necked frock she wears to the barbecue. The irony can't have escaped those left on the set: a marathon roll in the hay had restored the actress to a dewy virginity.

Between these two takes, months had passed, an avalanche of self-made problems in a relatively short time: artists and craftsmen had been hired and fired, and problems with the screenplay more than once almost halted production.

To a degree that today beggars belief, Selznick was not just devoting his frantic yet perfectionist zeal to *Gone with the Wind* but was busy with a dozen other projects at various stages of preproduction, production, and release. He was overseeing the final cut on *Intermezzo* and the publicity campaign to launch Ingrid Bergman as an American (that is, Hollywood) star; he was arguing with his latest import, Alfred Hitchcock, over the shooting of *Rebecca* while the crafty Englishman was devising ways to outfox his producer (by shooting the film in his head, giving Selznick no extra footage to play around with).

Selznick wasn't alone: working on multiple projects was standard operating procedure: Victor Fleming directed *The Wizard of Oz* the same year, and Cukor *The Women*. Actors and craftsmen, too, made several films a year, and Selznick had assembled the best that money could buy. The supporting cast is one reason the film lives on in the imagination. In our head we can still hear conversations between marvelous character actors like Harry Davenport's Dr. Meade and Laura Hope Crews's Aunt Pittypat, or Crews and Eddie "Rochester" Anderson as Uncle Peter. Thomas Mitchell, playing older than his years (forty-seven) and more Irish than his roots (Elizabeth, New Jersey), brings the right touch of bloody Ireland to Gerald O'Hara, and Victor Jory is both menacing and oddly sympathetic as the overseer Jonas Wilkerson. Jane Darwell, who would play Ma Joad in *The Grapes of Wrath* the following year, is memorable as the busybody Mrs. Merriwether.

The craftsmen were at a level collectively that Hollywood has rarely seen before or since, nor do the official credits begin to cover the many top-notch artists who were involved but didn't make the final list, starting with Cukor and Sam Wood, proliferating to fifteen-plus screenwriters who worked at one time or another replacing or rescuing Sidney Howard's work.

Walter Plunkett, who'd designed the (award-winning) costumes for *Little Women*, went South and studied native antebellum dress, and Joseph B. Platt designed the interiors; both worked closely with William Cameron Menzies on devising color motifs for different scenes. Menzies is the unsung hero of *Gone with the Wind.* As art director, his contribution, which included supervising many of the other craftsmen and directing certain uncredited scenes, is harder to pin down. The inescapable fact is that thanks to him, this three-hour-and-forty-six-minute film, with an intermission and a sprawling canvas with serious and even abrupt shifts in tone, doesn't break into fragments or lose its way stylistically or thematically. (Hattie McDaniel is the film's other anchor and source of continuity: people come and go, die and depart, shift locale, but she remains an abiding presence.) Selznick, however much he might think he was the only one who possessed the whole film in his head, knew he needed a better eye than his to give his sprawling opus visual coherence and so hired the one man—Menzies—who could do the complete film in sketch form.

Menzies is not as well known as he should be because of the near-impossibility of pigeonholing him or reducing him to one title. He entered the business at a time when movies were a young and evolving medium, titles overlapping and imprecise. Indeed, "production design by . . ." had to be invented for *Gone with the Wind*, and that didn't cover Menzies's incalculable and uncredited contribution as second unit director. He was at various times in his career art director, production designer, head of the art department, producer, uncredited director, and director later of such science fiction films as *Things to Come* and *Invader from Mars*. He was both art director and production designer of 1924's *The Thief of Bagdad* and uncredited director of the 1940 version of the same film. He had a hand in so many aspects of a film that we can only conjecture where his contribution ends and someone else's begins. He was responsible for "special production effects" for Hitchcock's *Foreign Correspondent*. Though not even listed as art director or production designer, his is considered by most film historians to be the visual imagination behind that movie's whimsically sinister sets and the terrifying climax when the plane crashes into the sea, a sequence that holds its own against all the technologically sophisticated "disaster" scenes and digital imagery of the past twenty years. In the twenties and thirties Menzies was one of the first to use storyboards and to appreciate the use of color for dramatic effect.

Technicolor wasn't brand-new: the revolutionary, wildly cumbersome three-color process had caused a sensation when introduced in *Becky Sharp* at Radio City Music Hall in 1935. (Radio City was itself almost brand-new, having opened in 1933.) But Menzies understood like no one else how to get the most out of it. His grasp of the dramatic core of a scene and swift, sure translation of that excitement into visual terms can be seen in his storyboard sketches, a fascinating contrast to those made by the other staff artists. Theirs are quite beautiful, painterly, detailed, *exquisite* tableaux, but Menzies's work—stylized, almost cartoonish—leaps off the page. In bold, broad strokes, with danger and violence cued strategically to color and composition, he uses a visual shorthand to heighten drama through shadows and light and the balance of color rather than fussy details. You could say Menzies's is the hand behind the mise-en-scène. The expressionistic landscapes and character positionings designed by Menzies and his staff keep certain images as touchstones, in the forefront of consciousness—like the horse collapsing on the bridge, the fire in the background, the use of the moon. But if we remember these images, it's because of the characters, who, however spectacular the landscapes or sets, are always driving forward.

Another of the geniuses was Jack Cosgrove, who invented new techniques for using paint and glass—the painting of Twelve Oaks, a matte shot for the burning of Atlanta. And it was production manager Raymond A. Klune whose idea it was to reassemble the existing sets on the studio back lot for the burning of Atlanta, and Selznick who backed him up when others like Eddie Mannix warned it couldn't be done or was too dangerous.

Hobe Erwin, who'd done the sets for *Little Women* and was involved in early conferences on the movie's visual aspects, received no credit after he was replaced by Lyle Wheeler. Lee Garmes, who pioneered low-key lighting with Josef von Sternberg, was canned after seven weeks for photography that Selznick, who never went for subtle effect when a grand one would do, considered too dark. In the same vein, he went for "sweepingly romantic music" and told Max Steiner to "just go mad with schmaltz in the last three reels." In fact, the composer gave him incessant and richly textured sounds throughout. Following his usual practice of writing "themes," there is one for Scarlett, another for Melanie, and of course the Tara melody that later became the popular single "My Own True Love." The rest was a brilliant assemblage of Civil War songs—"Marching through Georgia," "Dixie," "The Bonnie Blue Flag"—and various Stephen

Foster tunes. It was Hollywood prestige music, perfectly fitting Selznick's idea of a score that could soothe, excite, tranquilize, or quiver according to the demands of the situation.

Sidney Howard was the eminently capable and official screenwriter, but Selznick managed to find time to interfere relentlessly. He'd chosen Howard, he wrote to Kay Brown, believing him and Ben Hecht to be "the two best writers" in the business not tied up with a studio because "you don't have to cook up every situation for them and write half their dialogue for them." Nine days later another telegram expressed satisfaction with the Sidney Howard deal but warned Brown to keep open "the time and availability elements." "I never had much success with leaving a writer alone to do a script without almost daily collaboration with myself and usually also the director." So much for Howard's gift for independent thinking. This was the beginning of Selznick's relentless campaign to get him to Hollywood . . . and edit and improve on his work. The veteran playwright and screenwriter (*Arrowsmith, Dodsworth*) had won the Pulitzer Prize in 1925 for *They Knew What They Wanted*. He was an urbane gentleman who hardly knew how to deal with Selznick's aggressive come-hither. He preferred staying in the East, on his Upstate New York farm, as far away from Hollywood and Selznick as possible. One student of screenwriters has found an "auteurist" attraction to rural themes in his work, which might have given him a particular feeling for Margaret Mitchell's world. In any case, the two wrote long and mutually admiring letters as he worked on the script, and his death from a tractor accident just as the film was wrapping up was felt by the entire cast and crew as a blow akin to the start of the war.

Of the others who worked on the script, John Van Druten was called away from *Intermezzo*, to be followed by F. Scott Fitzgerald. His main contribution—not unimportant—was to criticize the existing script and excise extraneous dialogue. He cut a whole dialogue scene between Ashley, Scarlett, and Melanie whose import could be conveyed by looks alone. He laughed about Selznick's reverence for the text, writing to his editor, Max Perkins, "I was absolutely forbidden to use any words except those of Margaret Mitchell, that is, when new phrases had to be invented one had to thumb through as if it were Scripture and check out phrases of her's [sic] which would cover the situation!" Yet he gave one of the fairest summations of the book's virtues when he wrote to his daughter, Scottie, that it is "not very original, in fact leaning heavily on The Old Wives' Tale, Vanity Fair, and all that has been written on the Civil War . . . but on the other hand it is interesting, surprisingly honest, consistent and workmanlike throughout, and I felt no contempt for it, but only a certain pity for those who consider it the supreme achievement of the human mind." In the end, he came to respect both her and her dialogue.

Mitchell was of course in awe of Fitzgerald. She even thought she and her mother might have picked him up one day at Camp Gordon, where they would haul soldiers to town whenever they went to see Stephens. "After he got famous and I saw his picture

I remembered him." Might she not also have seen something of herself in Fitzgerald's protagonist Amory Blaine, a bright young thing who had a hard time fitting in or wanting to fit in: impulsive, fresh, egotistical, awkward, unpopular, conceited, slightly déclassé (Irish), and a lover of such lost causes as Bonnie Prince Charlie and the Confederacy? In any case, it seems appropriate somehow that these two sensibilities should converge in a process and a place that both of them resisted and longed for in equal parts. Also a little sad that Fitzgerald wound up at the end of his career doctoring a script for a Georgia belle not entirely unlike the Alabama one he'd married, attempting to write a scene for Rhett and Scarlett, trying it out on Sheilah Graham. By this time, Zelda was in the sanatorium, he was living with Graham, desperately in need of work, drinking, and depressed. To stimulate his imagination, he and she acted out scenes between Scarlett and Rhett, he who, once upon a time, had exerted his own Rhett-like fascination for women.

Fitzgerald was still working under George Cukor when Cukor's days were numbered; and Fitzgerald got fired, according to one biographer, for trying and failing to dramatize, under Selznick's command, Miss Pittypat *bustling across a room*. Others who worked on the screenplay at one time or another were John Balderston, Michael Foster, Oliver H. P. Garrett, Ben Hecht, Barbara Keon, Charles MacArthur, John Lee Mahin, Edwin Justus Mayer, Winston Miller, Donald Ogden Stewart, and Jo Swerling. One of the most tantalizing names never to have made it onto the official unofficial list is Howard Hawks. The master of screwball claimed in an interview in *Cahiers du Cinema* that he contributed dialogue during the Victor Fleming phase, and indeed the Hawksian ghost seems to hover behind the bickering eros of some of the Scarlett-Rhett scenes. Finally, stubbornly and most obstructively, there was Selznick.

At home, it was, as Irene Selznick wrote, like "being under siege. We were in a war and we were in it together." His shrewd, savvy wife was a powerhouse in her own right. In a different era she would have taken over MGM from her father, and she did go on to produce Tennessee Williams on Broadway. Together Irene and David watched the rushes each day, she serving as his closest adviser and sounding board throughout the production.

As the length became an issue, the producer briefly considered turning it into two films, then a long one with two intermissions. The cost kept going up. He was hoping to make it for two or two and a half million dollars. When it had climbed to a little under three and a half million, he wrote to MGM executive and Loew's vice president Howard Dietz on the necessity of special handling for "the longest picture ever made," one he hypothesized might gross ten, thirteen, or even fifteen million dollars. In what sounds like a cri de coeur, he continued, "I know all this sounds like Hollywood insanity to you, but if these expectations and hopes are insane, then I have been insane in the manner in which I have approached the picture (which I grant you is possible), because I have staked everything on it, including my personal future and the future of my company." (Costs eventually came to $4,250,000, exclusive of prints and advertising.)

The same visceral preference for the broad over the subtle, for sweeping drama over the fine-tuned gesture, underlay most of Selznick's tensions with his crew and craftsmen as well as the hirings and firings. Howard's tendency toward understatement, toward polite, oblique conversations rather than head-on collisions; Cukor's slow tempo, his perfectionist attention to gesture. Miniaturist (feminine) detail versus grandiloquent (masculine) sweep: these were the twin poles of David Selznick, of *Gone with the Wind*'s aesthetic, and the miracle is that one never quite usurped or prevailed over the other but both were held in uneasy equilibrium.

Ben Hecht, the go-to man for quick and brilliant rewrites, summoned by David, flew in for pots of money, then fled in two weeks, on the verge of a nervous breakdown. Selznick seemed to hold himself together by causing such nervous breakdowns in those around him. In that brief period, Hecht's main contribution was to persuade Selznick to keep most of Sidney Howard's script, but the modus operandi as described by Hecht provides a humorous glimpse into David's hands-on methods. Since Hecht hadn't read the book and was proud of it, Selznick and Victor Fleming forced him to sit up for all-night marathons, fueled by David's speed diet (Dexedrine, peanuts, and bananas), while they enacted the story for him, Selznick playing Scarlett and Ashley, Fleming Melanie and Rhett.

Where women were concerned, David-as-womanizer was perhaps the least complicated and least urgent side of the producer's nature. If not on the level of the great women's directors and producers like Josef von Sternberg, Max Ophüls, and Ingmar Bergman, he shared with them a richly ambidextrous mix of desire and identification. He certainly understood ordinary male lust, and he amply demonstrated, in both his movies and his life, the need to possess that ordinarily turns women into objects; but this was offset by an uncanny affinity with women, their sensibilities, their wardrobes, their special virtues and defects. In *Gone with the Wind* he showed an almost fetishistic attention to details of clothing. At one point in a frantic letter to Margaret Mitchell he asked, "How should we tie Mammy's bandanna?" to which she replied, "I don't know, and I'm not going out on a limb over a headrag."

When Mammy worked on Scarlett's waist, he insisted on amplifying the bosom to the measurements appropriate to historical romance. He got the best people for the job, then overrode them. "There's only room for one prima donna on this lot, and that's me." Yet as Olivia de Havilland attested, he had an "astonishingly unifying influence," was an "autocrat, but also charmer and enthusiast."

Tensions had been building between George Cukor and the producer from before the start of shooting: Cukor resented Selznick's interference in the screen tests, and then, after the film began, his constant rewrites, handed in each day and invariably inferior to both Howard's work and the book itself, while Selznick had become annoyed at Cukor for refusing to work on other pictures while *Gone with the Wind* was in preparation and was now finding his method too slow and finicky, too meticulous for the tempo of an epic. The great scene between Mammy and Scarlett was Cukor's work; the director even filled in an awkward gap by reintroducing dialogue from the book, to Selznick's great consternation. Indeed, the first scenes Cukor shot were straight out of the book: the opening on the veranda, the childbirth scene when Scarlett and a terrified Prissy deliver Melanie's baby; and the scene at Tara after the war when Scarlett shoots the Union deserter. But the delicacy of tone and gesture of Cukor's work would, Selznick felt, be ruinous if applied to the whole picture. One of the most disarming aspects of their relationship is their physical resemblance: they were as alike as brothers.

One of the few openly gay men in Hollywood, Cukor was known as a "woman's director," and in addition to Selznick's grievances, Gable, already deeply insecure about playing Rhett, was supposed to have made known his displeasure, reportedly with homophobic cracks. There was also gossip that Gable's past as a gigolo and possibly a rent boy made him nervous in Cukor's company. Gable didn't like Selznick, either, but Fleming was a director he trusted. They'd been friends since making *Red Dust*, the charmingly sexy pre–Hays Code movie with Jean Harlow and Mary Astor.

Barely days into the filming, Selznick informed the cast of the change. Leigh and de Havilland were horrified. They adored Cukor and begged and pleaded with Selznick to change his mind, but the producer was adamant. Leigh and de Havilland began a series of secret visits to Cukor on weekends, during which he would coach and rehearse them for their scenes. By this backdoor strategy, Cukor in effect continued to "direct," though without credit or portfolio. Later, Fleming had his own problems with the grueling schedule and pressures from Selznick, yet he could stand up to him in a way that the gentlemanly Cukor never could. He was foul-mouthed, blunt, and anti-Semitic to boot. When he looked at the footage, he went to the producer, according to Lee Garmes, and said, "David, your fucking script is no fucking good." A former racing car driver and mechanic, Fleming had come into movies as a stuntman and had earned his laurels as a director. He helped make Gary Cooper a star with *The Virginian* and again, in the early thirties, Jean Harlow with *Red Dust* and *Bombshell.* He was directing *The Wizard of Oz* (ironically, also as a replacement), and though he would win the Oscar for *Gone with the Wind, The Wizard of Oz* is the one film credit usually affixed to his name. Because of the combined pressures, he actually left the production for a brief period and fled to his Malibu house officially suffering from a nervous breakdown, and journeyman Sam Wood took over his chores. But if Selznick was in some sense the "real" director, Cukor and Fleming are the indispensable yin and yang of *Gone with the Wind,* their influences seen in the film's dual strengths—the bold, sweeping movement through time and history and the delicate gradations of feeling between lovers and family.

Selznick biographer Ron Haver describes Fleming's rough treatment of Leigh as an attempt to make her "Gable's kind of girl," but that was precisely what Leigh's Scarlett wasn't and would never be and why, in submitting, in adjusting to that proud, unpossessable creature, Clark Gable gives us, and gives up, something of himself we had never seen before—and would never see again. Gable had no illusions about his acting abilities, and he knew that Rhett Butler wasn't a part that played to his comfort zone. In terms of his career, he had as much to lose as Selznick in a role that would require both greater range and more humility than he'd demonstrated before.

The jug-eared actor had become the symbol of a kind of easygoing amused and amusing virility, an image carefully nurtured by the best talents in the studio system. Gable had arrived at MGM at a time, the beginning of sound, when silent stars like John Gilbert and Ramon Novarro were fading, and the studio desperately needed a new romantic male star. Excited by Gable's he-man possibilities, Metro executives called in Howard Strickling. Makeover maestro and publicist extraordinaire, Strickling was in effect Gable's Pygmalion. Drawing on the studio's dazzling array of artificial enhancements, he supervised the fixing of the teeth and the restyling of the hair, emphasizing the dangling cowlick, while the "brutish eyebrows, reminiscent of boxers Jack Dempsey and Max Schmeling," as biographer Warren Harris calls them, "were shaped and plucked to more debonair proportions." By turning the willing newcomer into a star, Strickling's work had just begun: for the length of Gable's career, he had to protect the King from the scandals and messes his newly charismatic self fell heir to.

Gable had always been drawn into relationships with older women who would become lovers, patrons, wives, or some combination thereof. There now came into his life possibly the most important of these, the renowned journalist and novelist Adela Rogers St. Johns, a sponsor who would also be an enduring fan. After meeting him, she pushed MGM to cast him in the adaptation of her racy novel *A Free Soul*. Eye candy and fetchingly naughty as a good-time gangster lover, he seduces good-girl Norma Shearer and almost steals the picture. He was at his ease on the screen with trashy dames like Joan Crawford and Jean Harlow (pairings that always implied the mutual recognition of shady pasts: both were "Gable's kind of girl"). But he also held his own with cool, ladylike types, Myrna Loy and Mary Astor, or, deliciously, Claudette Colbert in *It Happened One Night*—all actresses who conveyed banked fires beneath great surface aplomb. (The one such pairing that didn't work was with the spiritually passionate and man-annihilating Garbo in *Susan Lenox*.) Harris points out that it was Fleming and his scriptwriter John Lee Mahin who came to understand that Gable was at his best playing the foil. When the actor would complain that Harlow's wisecracks weren't all that funny, Mahin explained: "Your expression when we cut to you—that's the funny thing. The audience doesn't really start to laugh—doesn't really get it—until that big kisser of yours comes on and you're terribly uncomfortable or sore." Mahin also understood that Gable's appraising looks weren't leers, weren't filthy in any way, but were "frankly admiring. A woman never feels bad when she's told that she's got a lovely body, and that's what his eyes said."

This was the iconic Gable, and one tampers with an icon at one's peril. Most stars, for instance, refuse to play sex scenes in which they come a cropper. A famous male pinup of the seventies reportedly refused to play a scene in which he was supposed to turn to the woman, a megastar, with whom he'd just had a first sexual encounter and say, "It'll be better next time." When a star makes love, it's by definition perfect; the earth always moves. Gable, used to easy conquest on screen, was uneasy with a role in which the heroine didn't always love him. He complained, according to Harris, "It's the first time that the girl isn't sure that she wants me from the minute she sets eyes on me."

This was why he had resisted taking the part and why the relationship with Carole Lombard helped ease him into it. His great love, the wonderfully straightforward and uninhibited actress had transformed his life, given him new confidence, urged him forward when he held back. Maybe Lombard, adoring and believing in him, made up for the heroine who wasn't mad for him—though from all reports, Leigh, sensing his nervousness, went out of her way to relax him.

And then Fleming was what the apparently blasé but deeply insecure actor needed, the man in his corner on the set. As Rhett Butler, Gable retains everything that had made him "the King": the swagger and the irony, the charm and the twinkle, the virile presence. But the addition to the performance, paradoxically, is what's left out. Knocked out of him by the self-possessed Scarlett is that reflexive cockiness that sees all women as basically the same, all in need of a good lay. Until *Gone with the Wind* Gable's persona is based on a charmingly seductive caveman approach, an appeal to the atavistic urges papered over by custom and co-quetry. He can read a woman's desire at first glance. When she makes a pass at resisting, he gives her the look that says, "C'mon, who are you kidding, you know where we're headed!" a look that had to say all of that during a time when dialogue could say none of it. Now, faced with a woman who offers genuine, not pro forma, resistance, who's not telegraphing her attraction with each protest, a tiny crack in the King's confidence appears, a tremendously appealing shadow of doubt. He still thinks she needs a little rough handling, and we think so, too. But that's not the whole story, and Gable's willingness, as actor in character, to cede some of the automatic assurance for a more tempered and rueful approach is what makes his performance so unexpectedly lovely. If Fleming tried to make Leigh "more of a bitch," he allowed Gable to be less of a bastard. Perhaps without Fleming, his man's man of a director supporting and guiding him, Gable might never have relaxed enough to expose the vulnerable side of himself. There was the powerfully emotional scene following Scarlett's miscarriage in which Rhett was supposed to cry, and Gable desperately didn't want to do it. After much argument, Fleming persuaded him to try it both ways, do the scene with and then without tears, and they'd use the one he liked. He did it, and it was beautiful. Would he have done it for another director, for Cukor? Probably not. Actors vary, need different kinds and degrees of guidance, respond differently to different directors. A sense of security allows them to bring out qualities and nuances that might have remained forever submerged.

This inevitably came into play in the long series of missed signals and botched opportunities for reconciliation toward the end of the movie, one of the most agonizing lovers' quarrels in film or literature. It begins with her banning him from the bedroom, an act that in the movie is reduced to the relatively trivial issue of pregnancy avoidance to prevent the expansion of the famous wasp waist. In the book, it's clear that Scarlett, in one of two fateful meetings with Ashley at the mill, has suddenly been given reason to believe he loves her. His accusation that Rhett has coarsened and abused her, however untrue, gives her the idea. To remain faithful to this shadow lover, she orders Rhett permanently out of her bedroom, promising to lock the door. From this point on, the movie is vastly superior, a swift, stunningly violent love-hate duet, with blunt, gorgeous equivalents for the book's wordier and more genteel dance of separation. To show that nothing would stop him if he wanted her, Gable kicks the door down on his way out, a frightening harbinger of the rage and desperation that will lead him to the point of nearly killing her. In the drunken scene, foreplay to the rape and more terrifying than any horror film, his huge hands surround her neck, then move up to grasp her head in a hammerlock. He longs, he says, to crush it "like a walnut," to squeeze Ashley out of her mind and heart. Gable, less of a know-it-all than the book's Rhett, is shattering here, giving us a man who, for all his strength, his power and sophistication, is rendered utterly helpless by love.

From then on, up and down those stairs, through the rape, the pregnancy and miscarriage, Bonnie's death—every time she relents, softens, and smiles, he either doesn't see it or mocks her. Every time he reaches out, she closes down, gets that hard look on her face. Blind pride, drunken frustration, terrible timing are responsible, but most of all, a failure of empathy on the part of Rhett, the one whose empathy has until now kept the relationship afloat. He has always been able to enter into Scarlett's consciousness, she never into his. He's been able to compensate for her tone-deafness to the language of love and its unspoken signs. On the other hand, his very insight is a mark against him where she's concerned: he understands her too well; his clear-eyed view of them both as soul mates in greed and self-interest reflects back to her vision of herself that she—or the conscience of Ellen in her—can't bear.

When the book came out, one of the repeated criticisms even among the most favorable reviewers was that the weakest character was Rhett, that he was a "stereotype." Mitchell argued that both pictures and documents showed there were many such men in the antebellum South, but that was hardly the point. Rhett was something other than a stereotype—a label often trotted out when readers or viewers can't figure out what to make of a character. They wanted to fit him into the taxonomy of old-fashioned melodrama, a leering, mustachioed rogue, a swashbuckler of Victorian fiction. No, Rhett Butler was something else—an almost impossible fantasy, and one for which readers and audiences of the thirties had few models or reference points: a lusty, virile man who also appreciates a smart, challenging woman.

The fact that he buys Scarlett Paris fashions, knows women's clothes, has led one friend to argue that he's really a gay man in disguise, possessing an intuitive understanding of women's interests, the perfect confidant. Yet it's precisely because he's a "real man" whose masculinity (unlike that of a gay man) could be threatened by Scarlett that his attraction to such a powerhouse woman is all the more appealing . . . and extraordinary. By definition, a homosexual has nothing to fear (for example, rejection, sexual humiliation) from a beautiful and bewitching woman, whereas a heterosexual man does. The gay man is already *hors concours*, castrated, so to speak. It's a breathtakingly tricky balancing act. Just try to imagine Rhett played by a less virile actor, one of the early candidates such as Basil Rathbone or Ronald Colman, and you see how the movie loses its erotic steam, the chemistry that is its raison d'être. Fortunately Selznick paid no attention to Margaret Mitchell's protest, on behalf of all Southerners, at the purported casting of Gable.

Clark Gable "has never been the choice for Rhett down here," she wrote Kay Brown, after conveying disapproval of Norma Shearer as Scarlett ("too much dignity and not enough fire"). Gable "is not as popular here in the South as in other sections of the country—in tough and hardboiled roles, yes; but in other roles, no." Of course, she hastens to add, "People think he is a very fine actor, too, but they think he does not look Southern or act Southern and in no way conforms to their notion of a Low-Country Carolinian. In looks and in conduct Basil Rathbone has been the first choice in this section, with Fredric March and Ronald Colman running second and third." But wait . . . is this the same woman who introduced the tall, dark, and handsome stranger at the Wilkes's barbecue as "swarthy as a pirate"? The man whose muscles ripple, whose eyes glisten threateningly . . . ? Hardly the epithet one would apply to those three pale-faced drawing-room dandies! And the whole point of Rhett is his deviance from Low Country aristocracy, in looks and behavior.

It's part of her divided soul and forked tongue: the one-time rebel and porn reader, now impeccable Southern lady, apologizing to her confederates for her rebellious surrogates; taking back with her hypothetical casting the outlaw mystique to which the novelist has given full rein.

Whatever their official choice for the role of Rhett Butler, Mitchell and her compatriots had instinctively, like the rest of the country, cast Clark Gable. Rhett's "abrupt physical impact, something in the impertinence and bland mockery of his dark eyes," and several other bodice-ripping descriptions of physical passion were what reviewers no doubt had in mind when they called Rhett a stock figure of melodrama. In truth, the pulpishness of the descriptions reeks not of melodrama but of women's romance, a genre which *Gone with the Wind* more often and happily transcends. But the lurid poster with the torn, off-the-shoulder white shirt and rippling muscles, the profile in crimson glow, is straight out of the book, as is the kiss "with slow, hot lips." ("The muscles of his big body ripped against his well-tailored clothes . . . .") The beauty of Gable is that he could both embody and modulate this swashbuckler of love into something less purple and more ironic. It's just possible to imagine the other three candidates as elegant Southern renegades, but not as lust-and-love-crazed husbands. Nor would they convey the inherent paradoxes of a very masculine hero with such "feminine" qualities as an interest in women's fashion and tenderness toward children. And toward Scarlett. For the subtextual dimension of Rhett is not gay confidant but surrogate mother . . . the kind of mother that neither May Belle the suffragette nor Ellen the do-gooder could ever be. After the childbirth scene, when Rhett arrives to rescue them, he meets a distraught Scarlett at the gate. "I want my mother!" she wails heartbreakingly, and he enfolds her in his arms.

No less "maternal" are the emotions he displays for little Bonnie before and after her death. His delight at the baby, despite its being female, goes against the Southern custom of primogeniture and is what finally breaks the ice in his relationship with Mammy. And his devastation at her death calls forth a grief (he is supposed to become "unmanned") that he himself called "the only scene in his career where he could be called an actor." Maybe a maternal quality was always there, in the gentle protectiveness under the snappy brashness of the newspaperman in *It Happened One Night.* In any case, the combination of strength and vulnerability of Gable's performance was every bit as important to the film, to its sexual dynamics, as Leigh's. And let us not forget, as Mitchell in casting director mode seems to have done, the importance of his strength. For Rhett is in many ways a passive character, a reactor to Scarlett, but Gable's virility and star ego give the character the appearance of agency; his inherent masculinity can bend without breaking under the heroine's emasculating drive.

With Fleming and Cukor, the cast of *Gone with the Wind* had it both ways, were the beneficiaries of both one director's finesse and fine-tuning and the other's bold, no-nonsense approach to action. The deeply tragic sense of loss, of missed opportunities and cross purposes in the last half of the film wouldn't be so incredibly wrenching if we weren't pulling so powerfully—and illogically—for both of them. We want someone to at last quiet her fears, someone who truly understands her, who will love her enough to teach her to understand and appreciate his value. We want his feminine side to allow her to relax into her masculine side. A hopeless illusion, perhaps, but the magnetism of the two actors keeps us caught in the net of the illusion, a stand-in for all the hopeless, having-it-all yearnings of our young lives. We are as in love with them as a couple as Scarlett is stubbornly in love with Ashley, as hungry for anything that will feed the illusion, as dismissive of all the signposts that undermine and expose it. This terrifying and even corrupting power, this desperate star magic, is what literary men like F. Scott Fitzgerald leave out of the equation. Of all the writers who brushed pens with Hollywood, Fitzgerald was the least snobbish, the one most alert to the medium's possibilities. But even he failed to appreciate the make-or-break element of star magic at the heart of cinema, the way performances depend on writing and direction but finally call to us from their own sphere of sorcery.

Take the antipathy toward Scarlett: this was something Leigh anticipated, which is why she locked horns with Fleming over his one-dimensional view of her character. She would insist on shadings that would make Scarlett, if not more sympathetic, at least more complex, more varied. Working significantly in her favor, or at least modifying the way we see her, is the all-important love and forgiveness of people *we* love or at least trust. Not just Ashley but Rhett, Mammy, and Melanie—three characters with moral authority—love and admire Scarlett not in spite of but *for* her shrewdness and honesty, even her outrageousness. The same principle operates in *Jezebel*, with Fay Bainter's rueful love, as Aunt Belle, of Julie Marsden at her most vixenish softening our own exasperation with the termagant belle. Or in more recent years we can see Meryl Streep, playing abrasive characters in *Silkwood* or *Out of Africa*, softened in our eyes by the men who love her.

Surely the magic of Leigh and Gable was midwifed by both directors and would have failed had Fleming been as crude as his detractors have made him out to be. Olivia de Havilland, the last surviving member of the star quartet, provides insight into both in a Turner Classics DVD documentary that is part of a four-DVD Warner Home Video. Cukor, when he and she first discussed the playing of Melanie, said, "You have two choices. You can be pretty or plain," to which she replied, "Plain." Of course, she's the loveliest of plain, with exactly the hair (a carefully composed widow's peak) and dress of Melanie. Not quite the pale, sickly creature of the book or of Scarlett's malignant imaginings, nevertheless she's a subdued presence, stopping distinctly short of glamour. If she has little of the spark of her movies with Errol Flynn, her serenity has its own mysteries.

Not only Cukor but Selznick paid meticulous attention to Melanie's dress. She had only two beautiful costumes, de Havilland lamented—her one regret. In an early fitting of one of them, the designer had supplied four ruffles at the bottom of the skirt, one too many, she thought. She went, as was customary, to show it to Selznick. He examined it thoroughly, gave it the okay, then, as she was leaving, he called her back. "One ruffle too many," he said.

When she found that Cukor would be replaced by Fleming, she expressed her alarm to various people, among them Howard Hughes. "Victor has the same talent," Hughes told her, "it's just strained through a coarser sieve."

More surprising is de Havilland's revelatory insight into Fleming's sensitive side in a description that also shows the screenwriters' inventiveness when supplying something missing from the novel, in this case the scene when Ashley introduces Melanie to Scarlett in the grand foyer at the Twelve Oaks barbecue. In the book, no such scene exists: Melanie is introduced entirely through description, with a fever chart of Scarlett's reactions. A dialogue scene was necessary, and Selznick wrote a frantic and unsuccessful plea to Mitchell to write one.

The scene—de Havilland's first in the movie and first with Fleming—is a superbly orchestrated meeting of the three whose triangular relationship will be the core geometry of the movie. In the initial take, de Havilland says she descended the stairs and greeted Leigh graciously, but with the ritual politeness of a Southern lady.

"Stop," Fleming said, and approached her. "Whatever Melanie says, she *means*. She's not just polite. When Ashley says 'She's never insincere,' that's the key to her personality." De

Havilland said that was the most important bit of direction she was ever given, and after it she had total confidence in Fleming.

One senses in her performance what the actress confirms: that she loved the character of Melanie, that this utter sincerity was part of her fineness. She captures the inner security of a perfectly loving woman in a character that, though not multidimensional, is more interesting and enigmatic than her goody-two-shoes image might suggest. Her emotions are more steadfast than those of any other character, the first and most mysterious being that genuine and inalterable love of Scarlett, one of the reasons we accept Scarlett, too. Equally mysterious is her apparent ignorance of the bond between Scarlett and Ashley: does she really not see it, and is it that her own goodness blinds her to iniquity in others; is it a Christian resolve not to listen to gossip or think ill of those she loves; is she aware of the attraction but knows, as Scarlett does not, that it is she, Melanie, whom Ashley truly loves and needs? Or is it that all other emotions are overwhelmed by sheer gratitude to Scarlett, who honored her pledge to Ashley and with inhuman grit stayed behind in a burning Atlanta to help Melanie deliver her baby? In any case, her refusal to listen to gossip, to turn on or confront Scarlett, to allow herself to be attuned to the cross-currents of adulterous feelings, gives her a moral majesty that looks more interesting today than it did at the time. Having lived with the more dubious fruits of Scarlett's legacy, maybe it's time to take another look at Lady Melanie!

Even then, there were many—young girls as well as adults—who responded to Melanie, who really *did* take her for the heroine, preferred her to the morally distasteful Scarlett. As Rhett continually points out, she gives a depth of meaning to the word "lady," too often defined in only superficial ways. For Melanie's is not just the good of mindless conformity, of the path of least resistance (the simpering passivity that we young Scarlett-followers saw), but an active and hard-won integrity. When the chips are down, as in the stirring scene with the Yankee soldier (directed by Cukor), she shows herself as capable of grit and courage as her fearsome sister-in-law. Hearing the to-do, she arrives from upstairs, pale and unsteady with sword in hand. "I'm glad you killed him," she says, and as she does so, her eyes light up and her face flushes with a strange, un-Christian expression, an almost erotic glow of pleasure. The two women are joined momentarily in a mad, sisterly triumph, the exultation of women overcoming mortal danger without the help of men. Melanie, assuming control, heads off the others, saying the gun went off by accident. "What a cool liar you are, Melly," says an admiring Scarlett. Before figuring out how to dispose of the corpse, Melanie then suggests going through his pockets. "I wish I'd thought of that," says Scarlett, whose attitude toward her sister-in-law changes from that moment on. She can't completely let go of the reflexive contempt—it is too enmeshed with her attachment to Ashley—but the feeling is tempered by awe before a courage that is sister to her own. Indeed, if Melanie's love of Scarlett is one of the anchors of our own sympathy for the incorrigible heroine, the progression of Scarlett's feelings for Melanie, from jealousy and contempt to respect, appreciation, and finally love, is one of the most powerful themes of the movie. The evolution of the two women's relationship, the drama of Melanie's affection and Scarlett's resistance, constitutes a love story every bit as intense in its own way as Scarlett and Rhett's.

Another small Cukor masterpiece is the childbirth scene. Watch the expressions on Leigh's face as it emerges from the shadows. The filmmakers were also having to deal with Hays Office injunctions against showing too much agony and suffering in the process of childbirth. On whose behalf was the squeamishness? Women who then might decide not to have babies? (That was the expressed concern of the hugely influential Catholic Church.) Or men who relish bloody battle scenes but can't take the raw horrors of childbirth?

But a Fleming scene that can't be bettered, combining gusto and high-wattage chemistry and improving on the book, is the first dialogue scene between Scarlett and Rhett, when they meet in the parlor of Twelve Oaks. After Scarlett, in a fit of jealous frustration after Ashley has rejected her, throws and breaks a china figurine, Rhett's handsome head emerges, the serpent in the Garden of Eden, over the back of the settee.

"Has the war started?" he asks, in a line that isn't in the novel, grinning, to her shock and fury. Their exchange, one of the great first-encounters in the movies, is a full-out screwball battle, arrows of dialogue flying, the molecules of attraction and repulsion bouncing back and forth on a collision course as replete with present and future danger as Scarlett with a porcelain shepherdess in hand.

Susan Myrick's dispatches from the set, as distinct from her more candid letters to Margaret Mitchell and journal entry, portray Gable as his fans wanted to picture him. She understands full well the desire to believe, knows readers and viewers will go more than halfway to see the Gable they want to see. No mention of bad breath or false teeth as she goes into swoons of delight over the actor in person, how handsome, dashing, courtly he is, a wonderful dancer, nothing about his problems with the Virginia reel or with the Southern accent he was supposed to acquire under her tutelage. According to Myrick, he would "anxiously inquire if his accent sounded right." And she tells him (and her readers), "When the Southern women hear you say 'warm' and 'charming' and 'sure,' they'll be eating out of your hands, I assured him, for his accent is decidedly on the side of the Deep South." They're like a youngster's letters home from camp, telling the parents what they want to hear. But in fact, their mutual failure with the Southern accent was converted into a masterstroke—if inadvertent—on Gable's part. At a certain point, he simply refused to do it, and the film and his character were far better for it, richer and more interestingly ambiguous. With the all-British trio Leigh, de Havilland, and Howard, what the movie didn't need was one more Anglo-flavored Southern aristocrat. The not-quite-placeable accent, along with Rhett's more cosmopolitan background, pragmatic politics, war-profiteering activities, and deep skepticism about the Southern cause, allows him to become a kind of honorary Yankee, someone who blends the best of both sides, hence a figure who deflects some of the antagonisms inherent in the conflict. He could almost be one of those Northern relatives or beloved friends whose existence made secession so difficult for many Southerners. As he takes the audience into and makes them share his love of Scarlett, he's an important intermediary, someone who crosses back and forth between hostile camps, lowering the temperature.

Taken apart, he's riddled with inconsistencies, but Gable makes Rhett's hybrid nature seamless in one of those pieces of cinematic magic that is so organic as to be unanalyzable, almost undetectable. We hardly notice Rhett's lack of a Southern accent, he just sounds like "himself," someone with the ability to seem both insider and outsider simultaneously (a quality he shares with Leigh's Scarlett).

But there's one enchanting moment when, if you listen closely, Gable suddenly lapses, or rises, into a Southern accent. It's after the birth of Bonnie, when Mammy, who's been an unbending opponent of Scarlett's rascally (war-profiteer, no-account) husband, finally comes round. It's when she witnesses and is smitten by the depth of this man's love for his child—and a girl child, at that! She at last dons the red taffeta petticoat he had given her as a "wedding present" and which she had hitherto refused to wear.

In the conversation that ensues, she brandishing the skirt, he thrilled at having at last won over this formidable woman, he falls naturally into a Southern accent, echoing hers. Gable and McDaniel had actually performed together in movies and already liked each other (he was outspoken in making sure the black actors were treated as equals on the set). A descendant of slaves but born in free Kansas, she also had the devil of a time mastering the Southern accent. Their duet is one of the most charming scenes in the film, with much of its irrepressible good feeling conveyed by the unconscious way their voices mimic each other.

If Gable managed to quell his fears and rise to the occasion, Leslie Howard was, if anything, even less enthusiastic about playing Ashley, and his indifference is apparent in his lackluster performance. He felt, rightly, he was too old, and not beautiful enough. (Color did him no favors: he looks younger and more beguiling the same year in the black-and-white *Intermezzo* with Ingrid Bergman.) Part of the problem, if problem it is, lies in the ambiguity of Mitchell's characterization of the aristocrat-scholar, with Ashley's airy metaphysics reflecting her own mixed feelings regarding her mother's bluestocking pretensions and her own deficiencies as a person of ideas. Scarlett's inability to comprehend his simplest philosophical musings speaks with a strangely perverse evenhandedness both to her obtuseness and to his impracticality.

Fortunately for Howard's performance, however, lackluster is to some extent what Ashley is all about. Though it could be read by those who were so inclined—like Scarlett, like certain teenagers—as irresistible aloofness. For make no mistake: though it may strike viewers today as sheer lunacy, Leslie Howard was hot in his own cool way, a turn-on who possessed qualities that were the opposite of, and for many at the time, superior to, Gable's.

For female viewers, one of the great luxuries (found so rarely in book or movie) was being called upon to choose between two delectable types of male. Where men might go to movies and choose between endless variations on the virgin and the whore, we now entertained heated arguments over Ashley versus Rhett. Possibly Walter Scott, more than William Thackeray, is one of the true fathers of *Gone with the Wind* (about his baleful influence on the Southern self-image and notions of class gallantry Mark Twain was properly scathing), so Ashley and Rhett were our Rowena and Rebecca, the wan and perfect blonde, the lustrous and passionate brunette. Ashley, whose supporters ran to shy girls and control freaks, and Rhett, for the less repressed and for bad-boy addicts. Depending on your point of view, Ashley (or Leslie Howard) was sensitive, poetic, and enigmatic—or wan and a wimp. Rhett/Clark Gable was sexy, virile, and funny or just crude and unmannerly. The outcome was a crucial barometer of taste that would reveal a great deal, possibly too much, about a girl's temperament and predilections. It's easier today to find a needle in a haystack than to find someone who's turned on by Leslie Howard or Ashley Wilkes, or even to understand what we saw in him. Plenty, I assure you. Howard was a huge star (heart-stoppingly attractive in *Pygmalion* in 1938), still exuding allure in revivals in the fifties, though more of a draw in my mother's day than mine: that angelic blondness, the way he dipped his head in sympathy, the suave, low voice that exuded reticence and refinement, Howard was the "It" gentleman of the rampant Anglophilia of which Hollywood was both addict and supplier. Selznick adored British royalty, was constantly drawn to stories of aristocrats tragically in love with commoners (see *The Prisoner of Zenda*), so no surprise that he was completely broken up (is reported to have shed real tears) over the abdication of Edward VIII to marry the divorcée (commonest of commoners!) Wallis Simpson. (Or that he populated the aristocracy of *Gone with the Wind* with British imports.) It was an age of repression, of sacrifice, *that* was the turn-on: so Ashley's noble hard-to-getness was as much an aphrodisiac to most of us as it was to Scarlett. Never mind that he was a shadow, an illusion, that we sensed the hollowness of a displaced soul from the beginning: isn't that what love was? Freudians would have gotten the message. A yearning for the unavailable, the unreal? Oh, yes, especially in the South, where we were both repressed and, not to be redundant, father-fixated. Safer to stay with the dream, in which father and suitor blended in the just-out-of-reach fantasy that movies gave form to, allowing us to live briefly in an ideal world of vaguely taboo romantic yearning without having to come to earth in favor of a real, and lesser, human connection. As potent carrier of the romantic virus, "My Own True Love" could apply to all that was lost but not really surrendered—that necessarily imprecise romantic yearning that floats suspended somewhere in a realm of the unconscious, meaning everything and nothing.

Only movie stars at their most otherworldly and magnetic in a darkened movie theater could provide such direct conduits to those adolescent passions too confused and forbidden to be disclosed in the light of day. And only on a Hollywood back lot could a producer achieve the idealized mythical South that Selznick wanted, the Confederacy that colonized our dreams, and gave a nation its enchanted past.

FIVE

Beautiful Dreamers

The year 1939 was a culminating moment of classical cinema. Sunlight and shadows were in equal balance, an equilibrium due at least in part to a sense of gender harmony, of male and female stars sharing the screen and getting along. It was a golden age in the sense that the studio system was operating in a world not yet overshadowed by a second world war and the Holocaust, not yet grown unduly pessimistic. In the forties and fifties, movies would grow darker and more ominous, the relationship between the sexes more strained. In noir and the woman's film, destructive or insidious women, pathological femmes fatales and boss ladies began to disturb the balance of power—embodying the very masculinization of the American woman of which Scarlett was such a deceptive foremother.

In 1939, the Couple—white, heterosexual, and WASP—was still

the godhead in the monotheism of romantic love, a twin deity that would soon be dethroned under the relentless pull of egalitarianism and the decline of the studio system. Women, heretofore the essential—and more revered—half of the couple, would be the major casualty. First would come the gritty solipsists of the Method, boy-men whose argument was with society rather than women. Then, in the seventies and eighties, a welcome influx of ethnic stars, but again, males predominated, with buddy duos taking over the sparring, screwball dynamic. Out of this emerged the horny slacker bonding dudes and the guy-flick/chick-flick standoffs of the present, along with the alpha male stars who continue to kick butt in superhero thrillers. But even the marquee names have ceded some of their specialness to the flood of human flotsam brought forth by the anti-iconic candid-camera aesthetic of everyone's-a-star on YouTube. The wide-open, unfiltered world of the Web is democracy's final revenge on Democracy. Ever ready for their close-ups, the assorted players barely bother to Photoshop themselves—that is, assume the facade of virtue and beauty that Alexis de Tocqueville pointed to as the inevitable overlay of a born-yesterday culture. When the great Frenchman observed that the handicraftsmen of democracy "strive to give all their commodities attractive qualities they do not really possess," he might have been looking into a crystal ball and seen Hollywood on the horizon.

Yet *Gone with the Wind*, for all its couple-based faith and smooth propulsion, is not without a note of uncertainty. If the book is America's Bible, where is it telling us to go, what to believe? What is America's role in a world on the verge of war: who are we, nationally and internationally? The conflict between two sections of the country, and between Northern and Southern values, lurks unresolved beneath the drama ("Appomattox settled nothing," Margaret Mitchell wrote to a correspondent), with little of the reconciliation theme evident in earlier Civil War pictures. Nor did *Gone with the Wind* offer much hope for truce in the war between the sexes.

Not unlike the star system of thirties Hollywood, 1860 was the culminating moment of the divine order of the colonial South, with the white male planter positioned just below God atop a hierarchy of race, class, and gender. What Vivien Leigh and Clark Gable—and Leslie Howard and Olivia de Havilland— were to ordinary struggling actors and actresses, the planters and their culture were to the rest of the South, a tiny elite idealized by some (the North), resented by others—the rest of the South. Those few families possessing more than a thousand slaves, the true slave-owning upper class, remained aloof and, in their relatively protected isolation, could afford a more cavalier attitude to slavery. The enlightened scions of the Old South—Mary Chesnut and her great friend, my ancestor Wade Hampton—could, like Ashley, be antislavery without in the least believing in racial equality. It would never have occurred to them to envision blacks on an equal footing. Theirs was a kind of benign paternalism: blacks should be freed but educated. As governor of South Carolina, Hampton was in favor of giving Negroes the vote and gradually assimilating them into white society. Their greater enemies were the rabble unleashed by Reconstruction ("worse than the war"): radical whites and reactionary Democrats who were closer economically to blacks and had more to fear from them.

■

During the romantic gloss of the South, the Civil War became a favorite theme, first during the 1870s, when war memorabilia were ubiquitous in the North and Robert E. Lee and other Confederate generals were the subject of best-selling lithographs. There had been novels of Southern pleading before the war, and after it plantation novels like those of Thomas Nelson Page, that set the tone of glorification that Allen Tate called the literature of narcissism rather than introspection. The South saw itself as the victim in a Trojan War, the "older" culture of Troy-South wiped out by the "upstart" culture of Greece-North.

Compromise over Western expansion of the slave trade had become impossible as the extremists had taken over—Abolitionists and radical Republicans in the North, fire-eaters and Bible justifiers in the South. All had God on their side. In the aftermath: guilt and atonement on the part of the North, rationalization and self-aggrandizing on the part of the South. The South was devastated by the war. Not only had the Union army invaded and conquered the South, but, as historian James McPherson points out, it had destroyed two-thirds of the value of Southern wealth: almost half of the livestock, more than half of the farm machinery, and most of the railroads and industries. On top of this, the South had lost a quarter of its white males aged twenty to forty. "Before the war, when cotton was 'king,'" writes McPherson, "the Southern average income was sixty-eight percent of Northerners; by 1870, it was thirty-nine percent, where it stayed for forty years." The North felt a certain guilt over its complicity in the slave trade—the trade from which the planters, despite their carefully cultivated image of being above the economic fray, had made a huge profit.

From a (partly false) sense of invincibility before the war, how was the South to account for the catastrophe? Southern planters had been the world's chief supplier of cotton by 1820, exporting more than three-fourths of the crop before the war. The argument over tariffs, a probative cause of the war, was real. Yet even before the war, in the midst of their balloon of irrational exuberance, Southerners were riding for a fall. The English textile boom was petering out, and the South had no manufacturing industry to speak of (the point Rhett Butler makes to the war-hungry Southern aristocrats). Add to this the inner conflict between a New South striving to catch up with the North (of which go-getter Scarlett O'Hara and the city of Atlanta were emblematic) and the recoil against Yankee values by backward-looking agrarians and other defenders of the Old South. These two sides could pretend to cohere in the embrace of a mythic past.

The narratives that came after the war took on a healing,

conciliatory tone. Parables such as Jules Verne's *The Mysterious Island* (1875) pitted the antique grace of Southern living against crass modernity. In that famous fantasy, five Richmonders and a presumably well-bred dog escape from the war in a balloon and are planted in a *Survivor*-style setting, with nature red in tooth and claw represented as an escape from the despised Industrial Revolution.

Movies of the Civil War followed, all evenhanded or even deferential in their portrayal of Southerners. Divisive issues were buried in favor of the celebration of heroes. Union brother and brother-in-law had fought against Southern brother and brother-in-law; West Point friends battled against each other; a great many Southerners of every rank were themselves divided, opposed to slavery but loyal to their patch of the South. Reconciliation meant something to these men wracked with ambivalence and to those brothers and friends turned foes.

With Appomattox and the courtesies extended between Lee and Ulysses S. Grant (Lee explaining why the soldiers needed to keep their horses; Grant graciously complying), the theme of nobility was consolidated into a warm glow of hagiography. The messiness of the war, the desertions, the disease (which carried off more men than gunfire did)—the trials of the ordinary soldier were buried in the ongoing emphasis on the generals, their feats, their strategies, and their eccentricities as protagonists of the official "novelistic" narrative, as Walt Whitman called it. The bleaker and more scathing portrayers of war—Ambrose Bierce,

John De Forest—or of the South—Ellen Glasgow—had little chance against the mythologizers.

War itself was thrilling and romantic . . . and male. Ashley, when Scarlett calls him heroic, contradicting his claim of cowardice, says tiredly, "That's not courage. Fighting is like champagne. It goes to the heads of cowards as quickly as of heroes. Any fool can be brave on the battle field when it's be brave or else be killed." And Rhett gets into trouble with Dr. Meade when he says, "All wars are sacred to those who have to fight them. If the people who started wars didn't make 'em sacred, who would be foolish enough to fight?" When he alludes to venality on the part of Southern soldiers, Dr. Meade reacts furiously against "slurs on the courage of the men in the field."

Robert Penn Warren understood that we don't want to remember a past full of defects; that we need a new image of the past in order to believe that even if we weren't "good and righteous before . . . we can be good and righteous today and tomorrow." The chief value of the past, he suggested, is as an inference, a creation. "In creating the image of the past we create ourselves and without that task . . . we might be said scarcely to exist."

Margaret Mitchell grew up within this myth, and forty years later, so did I. As a Virginian, my loyalties were more divided: I lived closer to the Mason-Dixon Line than Mitchell, and in addition, my paternal grandfather was a New Yorker. Margaret Mitchell, too, had relatives in the North, had visited and attended college there, but her heart belonged to the South. Richmond's Monument Avenue, along which I rode daily or weekly, was studded with Civil War generals and statesmen looming over and defining the present—perhaps poised to resume the as-yet-unfinished battle. These statues reminded us—lest we forget for a moment—that we belonged to and were ennobled by this tribe of cavalier heroes. And of course—this was the attraction of the Lost Cause mythology—we were grander, purer in defeat than were those crass, winner-take-all Yankees with their greedy industrial culture. The myth of the Lost Cause and the moral superiority of losing defined and fed our romantic sense of ourselves, our specialness, our region marked by a defeat that wasn't quite a defeat in a war that wasn't quite over. Margaret Mitchell, who acknowledged that in the South there were "more rules than any place in the world if one is to live in any peace and happiness," understood that you have to give up something of yourself for the demands and pleasures of belonging to the tribe. Shaped, and to some extent dwarfed, by a sense of the past, we recognize that we're not the beginning and end of things and so accept being partly submerged in our allegiance to the tribe. In Stark Young's *So Red the Rose*, which is all about the ascendancy of kinship over the individual and bloodlines and breeding as cornerstone to Southern civilization, a character arrives from out of town for a relative's birthday party: "See here, Sis Bedford," she says, "I get confused, . . . so many people, which is which?" And Sis Bedford, describing a culture that is really one extended family, says, "You know who they all are, if not who each one is . . .

you must take it all as one." Indeed, one of the singular astonishments of *Gone with the Wind* is how Mitchell manages to create such an abundance of major and minor characters, un-Southern individualists, black and white, and keep them straight in our eyes.

This sense of strong family ties and the drama of a house divided made the South a peculiarly appealing subject for Hollywood. In discussing the Civil War films favored by the early moguls in the teens and twenties, Bruce Chadwick in *The Reel Civil War* makes the point that as newly arrived European immigrants they knew and cared little for American history but wanted to give their adopted country a past they could be proud of, one that featured strong family values, in which women and children were honored. The desire to appeal to as many people as possible, most immigrants like themselves, along with a sense of their mission as the purveyors (and shapers) of American popular culture, fostered in moviemakers from the beginning a broad and conveniently malleable view of history. A kinder, gentler world than that of the North and the shtetls they'd left behind. Inventing an America for a disparate population, one thing they all had in common was family. Our sentimental nostalgia for family has created a strange double standard whereby the "likable family"—the Sopranos or the Corleones—is forgiven the most appalling behavior. For those early reinventors of the American past, Civil War films and the reconciliation theme were made to order.

The United States was a country short on history, after all, short on evolutionary *stages* of history, barely a country. So we looked like upstarts to the rest of the world? Well, here was proof that we weren't the only nation, as Georges Clemenceau is said to have remarked, that had "gone directly from barbarism to degeneration without the usual interval of civilization." Here was our civilization, our Middle Ages, our feudal past with modern graces thrown in.

That slavery itself might be a mark of barbarism was conveniently overlooked, and the South, of course, was guilty of what would come to be seen as the greatest sin of all. But in 1939, in the midst of the Jim Crow era, with lynchings still common in the South and guilty complicity in the North, we could still look without embarrassment on institutionalized racial inferiority as a "given."

As in Griffith's *Birth of a Nation*, where two friends are torn apart by the war, love between a Southern girl and a Northern soldier was often at the center. Shirley Temple was an instrument of reconciliation in *The Little Colonel* and a mediator between black and white in *The Littlest Rebel*. It was the importing of slaves that had caused all the trouble.

Underlying the appeasement of the South there was also the question of the legitimacy of the war, of Lincoln's forcing the issue of the Union. Wasn't he embracing America's messianic vision of itself (the interpretation Edmund Wilson proposes in *Patriotic Gore*)? Wasn't he implementing the very policies we deplore in present leaders, imposing union on a section of the country that in coming into existence through revolution had by all logic the right to secede and that saw secession as the next chapter in the revolution? In moral relativist terms, the South was really a sort of "third world," a premodern country of families and clans, bound by tribal bonds and antique concepts of honor and violence, thus not amenable to Republican ideas of government. At work is the inevitability of historic forces that we see in the Middle East, in European expansions of the nineteenth and twentieth centuries, in the novels of Walter Scott, so beloved by Southerners, reflecting the English victory over the Scots: that is, the tendency of a more industrial and diverse economy to colonize a weaker, agricultural one. Of a more educationally advanced culture (only 6 percent of the North's free adult population was illiterate in 1860, compared to 17 percent in the South) to dominate a more backward one. Each culture sees itself as superior and either sets out to impose its vision on other nations (in self-defense, in exploitation) or asks to be left alone, especially after a war when the South had been invaded and where Southerners were now unable to hold political office. The carpetbaggers who arrive in Georgia in *Gone with the Wind* (one white, one black, nattily dressed) are an insult almost beyond defeat; as Ashley remarks, "Reconstruction is worse than death."

So the North turned a blind eye to Jim Crow, accepting the South's assertion that only white Southerners understood and could deal with their blacks. And sympathy for the South, namely the planter class, came from such unexpected quarters as H. L. Mencken and Edmund Wilson. The feudalism was, of course, only one small portion of the South, as Mitchell herself recognized. Among Southerners there was tremendous resentment of planters for stealing the limelight and credit from small farmers who'd fought in a war that wasn't theirs to begin with, who'd lost their land and relatives. The planters had, as Atlanta journalist Ralph McGill expressed it, aroused ire by "putting their stamp on the South." The deliriously intemperate W. J. Cash recognized, as did social commentator Thomas Sowell, the mixed ancestry and disparate nature of Southerners, their indebtedness to their culture of origin, the semi-barbarian Scotch and Irish clansmen of the seventeenth and eighteenth centuries. Sowell and Grady McWhiney (*Cracker Culture*) point to the Celtic background of so many Southern rednecks and crackers (so named in British Isles subculture), who preserved traits and brought to America what Sowell calls "a whole constellation of beliefs and attitudes that would be counterproductive." There were qualities shared, whether admitted to or not, by both whites and blacks: an aversion to work, an excess of pride, a tendency to violence, a sensitivity to personal slights, a contempt for book-learning and education, and a fidelity to guns, religion, and tobacco.

The Southern aristocracy, enclosed in its own lofty world, moved to a different rhythm. If the planter class was anachronistic at the outset of war, it was doubly so afterward. As Robert Lively says in *Fiction Fights the Civil War*, the Natchez aristocrats of *So Red the Rose* were "no believers in slavery [but] did nothing to abolish it." They swept to the defense of the Confederacy despite rather than because of the shrill hysteria, "were too polished for fierce anger, too honest for self-righteousness, and so much an institution that the war's harshest blows failed to shake their stability."

Gone with the Wind is like a house of mirrors, reflecting the ironies evident to someone like Mitchell who grew up within segregation, a culture shaped by an institution, slavery, that was putatively dead. A culture that, despite the valedictories ("gone with the wind" or, as a caption from *Birth of a Nation* has it, "a way of life that is to be no more"), was in fact much the same in feeling, in clinging to the rites and rituals of an aristocracy, in relegating blacks to a "separate but equal" sphere that was definitely separate—and anything but equal. Mitchell had her own conflicts, typical of the time. At Smith, she asked to be removed from a class in which a Negro student was present, yet in other ways she showed an openness toward black aspirations, was extremely close to her black housekeeper, and studiously tried to capture black patterns of speech. She was guilty of coarse and reflexive racism in her life and in some of the book's language, yet there are genuinely subversive strains in the book, and Mitchell dragged her feet and pen as a result. Her concern about the reaction of the home folks proved unnecessary; there's nothing like success to becalm the local impulse to find grievance and slander. But it might have been otherwise: as Medora Perkerson, her friend and editor, said, "Wasn't her heroine a baggage, with nothing to recommend her but courage? And wasn't her hero a scoundrel, who profiteered at the expense of the Confederacy? And didn't her book contain the shameful truth that there were some deserters from the Confederate Army?" And that, as Ashley admitted, "things aren't as bad in Yankee prisons as they are in ours" and that "we Southerners did think we were gods."

At the bazaar for the Confederate hospital, the women blaze with an ecstatic and transfiguring patriotism that leaves Scarlett both envious and skeptical. Their delusions about victory, their dismissals of the deaths, makes her wonder if that wasn't "too high a price to pay for such a Cause?" In seeing the war through the eyes of the women, the movie, like the book, is genuinely antiwar, showing the conflict between patriotism, with its obligation to support the warrior cause, and the dread of losing beloved husbands and sons. Perhaps this is the only way to make the case against war, because once you move to the battlefield, the fascination with violence takes over. Modern man, as William James argued in his great essay "The Moral Equivalent of War," inherits "all the innate pugnacity and all the love of glory of his ancestors." In 1906, James anticipates every "antiwar film" to come: "Showing war's irrationality and horror is of no effect on him.

The horrors make the fascination. War is the *strong* life; it is life *in extremis;* war taxes are the only ones men never hesitate to pay, as the budgets of all nations show us."

■

As soon as plans to make the film were announced, blacks had begun to agitate and protest. David Selznick wanted to enlist their support—after all, he remembered the huge furor over *Birth of a Nation*—but he would go only so far. He declared himself, as a Jew, sensitive to issues of prejudice, and for his time and place he was. As biographer Ron Haver says, "He was no bigot but he did subscribe to the prevailing liberal ethic of the time, which treated blacks with 'dignity' yet kept them in their place."

He was "bewildered" by the letters and protests, saying, "I feel so keenly about what is happening to the Jews of the world" and "the only liberties we have taken with the book is [sic] to improve the Negro position in the picture . . . very great friendship toward them and their cause."

Yet he had trouble understanding why the word "nigger" might be offensive to blacks. He cited the use of "wop" as a precedent, but Val Lewton gently persuaded him that there was a difference and that the word should be dropped. It was. At the same time, he refused to hire a black adviser, knowing he would expunge much of the humor (that is, Prissy).

Perhaps nowhere is the book or movie more vulnerable to criticism than in the treatment of Reconstruction. From 1865 until 1877, when federal troops were at last recalled from the South, there was a period of partial success during which former slaves voted, served on juries, were councilmen and magistrates. The South began the first system of public education, but you would never know it from *Gone with the Wind*. Or from *Birth of a Nation*. Or, for that matter, from the accredited histories of the period. The reigning view was of vast, unchecked corruption, of scheming blacks subverting legitimate government or shiftless blacks exploiting it; of carpetbaggers and scalawags taking advantage of disfranchised white Southerners; and of white Southerners being victimized both by armed local blacks and interfering federal troops. There were the lone and unattended voices of Frederick Douglass and W. E. B. DuBois, but Claude Brown's view of Reconstruction as the "Tragic Era" and William A. Dunning and his school of Southern apologist historians prevailed. Not until recent years have scholars like Eric Foner unearthed and brought to light the positive aspects of Reconstruction.

Margaret Mitchell does her part to perpetuate the slander. There are no Negroes who join the Union army, and afterward, none who vote or hold office. She shrewdly places her most scathing remarks in the mouth not of a white racist but of a disgusted Mammy, whose Atlanta is polluted by "free issue niggers." The threat of rape hovers everywhere. Selznick tones it down a bit, getting rid of the KKK in favor of a furtive "social club" to which the veterans and gentry belong. (In fact, Mitchell didn't want the KKK in the book originally, but her publisher encouraged her to include the Klan.) The midnight lynching is obliquely presented: a wounded Ashley is saved by Rhett while Melanie nervously and quietly keeps the ladies together by reading at the sewing circle. The violence was worse in states with black majorities: Mississippi, Louisiana, Georgia. This was also a time of corruption, on the part of blacks, whites, and everyone in between. Meanwhile, the Republican Party in the South was increasingly controlled by banking and commercial interests, and labor unrest was widespread in 1873. One problem was that blacks themselves were less interested in franchise than in farms. After all, in an agricultural era, land was the only means of supporting a family. Slaves knew how to farm, knew the land firsthand. Their sweat and labor as they pick cotton, the interludes of joy and singing, are accurately and movingly depicted in the opening scene of *Gone with the Wind* and in King Vidor's all-black masterpiece, *Hallelujah!* This was their world and their community, and quite naturally their longing to farm their own land was stronger than the desire for the vote.

The ninny Aunt Pittypat is in a constant state of hysteria over the possibility of rape or murder by "addled" darkies, but of the Negro vote she says, "Did you ever hear of anything more silly? Though—I don't know—now that I think about it, Uncle Peter has much more sense than any Republican I ever saw and much better manners but, of course, Uncle Peter is far too well bred to want to vote." Radical Republicans saw equality in terms of franchise. But Sherman's forty acres and a mule, a closely knit community of farms, was much closer to what Steven Hahn, in a review of Eric Foner's *Forever Free*, has called black "protonationalist and separatist tendencies" and what Negroes actually desired in 1865.

For her portrait of Reconstruction, Mitchell, usually a demon for historical accuracy, cites the published recollections of an "eyewitness," one Princess Agnes Elizabeth Winona Leclcrcq Joy Salm-Salm, the wife of a general with a name even slightly longer who served as military governor of Atlanta from July to October 1865. No doubt the princess's experiences and attitude provided the ammunition for a lengthy diatribe on the part of Scarlett, who paints a dire picture of abandoned Negro children, an overwhelmed Freedman's Bureau, whiskey-sodden Negroes, "the old darkies [going] back to the plantations gladly" but becoming a burden on planters, and Jonas Wilkerson, the ex-overseer, stirring up black men to rape white women. In an out-of-character moment, Scarlett muses, "Here was the astonishing spectacle of half a nation attempting, at the point of bayonet, to force on the other half the rule of negroes, many of them scarcely one generation out of the African jungles." The speech strikes a thoroughly false note, not the kind of observation you'd expect from our blinkered and not particularly civic-minded heroine but one you might anticipate from Mitchell in propaganda mode. But even here there are contradictions as Scarlett's demystifying impulses take over: her self-interested realization that she "has no legal rights, no legal redress," is more in character.

Then, in another op-ed diatribe, she paints a picture of "the peril of white women," lonely women, unprotected by men, vulnerable to rape. It's "the large number of outrages on women" and concern for their safety that "drove Southern men to cold and trembling fury and caused the Ku Klux Klan to spring up overnight." Yet moments later, Scarlett seems doubtful, even disapproving, when she describes an incident in which the Klan has seized a Negro who had "boasted of rape" and lynched him before he could be brought to trial, in order to spare the white victim from testifying in open court. The town understands that this is the only recourse since her father and brother would have shot her first, but when the military authorities react with fury, Scarlett wonders why "the crack-brained young fools in the Klan [didn't] leave bad enough alone and not stir up the Yankees like this? Probably the girl hadn't been raped after all. Probably she'd just been frightened silly and, because of her, a lot of men might lose their lives." Even if her skepticism springs less from Negro sympathies than from a dim view of her own sex, it's still evidence of Scarlett's healthy ability to see through the pieties and sanctimonies, the huffing and puffing of male braggadocio and honor killing.

The movie is more often than not an improvement over the novel, cutting Mitchell's long and repetitive descriptive passages, but the book boasts a rich assortment of supporting characters who amplify and contradict the fairly simple race relations of the movie.

One of the most moving scenes in the book, abbreviated to a few moments in the movie, has Scarlett giving Pork the watch that "Mist' Gerald" had left for him. He's appalled, insisting that it's "a w'ite gempmum's watch" and that it should be left to Wade Hampton, but she won't take it back.

"It belongs to you. What did Wade Hampton ever do for Pa? Did he look after him when he was sick and feeble? Did he bathe him and dress him and shave him?" She then offers to take it to be engraved, but he won't let her. Is he afraid she'll change her mind, she wonders? Then the light dawns. Does he think she'd sell it? she asks, to which Pork replies, "Yas'm—ef you needed the money."

> "You ought to be beat for that, Pork. I've a mind to take the watch back."
>
> "No'm you ain't!" The first faint smile of the day showed on Pork's grief-worn face. "Ah knows you—an' Miss Scarlett—"
>
> "Yes, Pork?"
>
> "Ef you wuz jes' half as nice ter w'ite folks as you is ter niggers, Ah spec de worl' would treat you better."

It's easy for someone who's never lived in the South to take a cynical view of this bond between black and white, but no one in good faith can believe it doesn't exist. Likenesses, in the form of rhythms, speech, a great many common virtues and defects, the caring that springs naturally from intimacy—these have to be acknowledged alongside the evils of slavery, chronic racism, and segregation. Under slavery, blacks and whites grew up alongside and intertwined with one another like vines on a tree, their roles mutually defined, their status mutually dependent. This affinity might have been clearer in one way (cluttered in another) if Southern writers had given their white characters, instead of standard grammatical English, the accented speech that is often closer to Negro dialect than to Northern speech.

The North of today, far from endorsing and colluding in the vision of a graceful class society built on slavery, distances itself completely from the antebellum South and from the tentacles of racism too threatening to claim for its own. If anything, we of the liberal post–civil rights North have been more invested in its other extreme, a vision of the South as intractably racist, integrated in name only. By demonizing the South as racist, we can disguise and also express our own prejudice. Also, by being horror-struck over prejudice in the South, Northern whites can distance themselves from their own taboo feelings of racial superiority. The more it became apparent that the North had its own racial problems and prejudices, the greater the need to see the South's as wholly other and pernicious, a difference in kind rather than degree. We (and here I align myself with my adopted home, the North) are in effect saying, You alone are guilty of these dark feelings and the crimes that come out of them: my outrage proves that I harbor no such prejudices, that I am not like you at all. This may be changing, but sporadically. During my forty years as a Southern transplant, I consistently found that any hint of harmony between the races, of family feeling, even of love between the races, would be met with disbelieving fury, dismissed as factitious, as lies the South tells about itself. Such complex truths are threatening because they undermine Northern liberal righteousness and challenge the demonizing of the South as a repository of pure racism from which Northerners are exempt.

Yes, Mitchell is guilty of portraying slavery with a happy face and is not particularly enlightened by contemporary lights. Her Negroes are also unacceptably passive, the blacks of *Birth of a Nation* showing a far more virile and aggressive side: with danger and menace came a whiff of black pride as well. With Mitchell, the taint of slavery was transmogrified into harmonious cohabitation, a hierarchy (another canny maneuver on her part) in which the white trash Slatterys were far more lazy, noxious, and parasitic than Negroes, especially the house "darkies," who look down on the field hands, who in turn look down on shiftless, no-account "niggers" wherever they're to be found. At the same time, *Gone with the Wind* contains unusually finely drawn portraits of blacks who are given voices, humor, importance.

Mammy is, of course, the presiding genius, the soul of the family, its jealous guardian, Scarlett's conscience and scold, the only one who understands *and* stands up to her. She's a conservative force, much like the black housekeeper, cook, and guardian whom Mitchell employed for most of her adult life, who believed, and preached to Margaret, that a woman's place was beside, and inferior to, her husband. Prissy comes to Scarlett as a gift from her mother, Dilcey, the tall, beautiful, half-Indian slave who doesn't make it into the movie. Dilcey's innate dignity, acquired in the blood, surpasses even Mammy's. Her daughter is another matter. "She's a sly, stupid creature," says Scarlett, in the vein of takes one to know one. Prissy, with her whining, lying ways, is a stumbling point for most viewers, yet the humor and wild individuality she brings to the movie is a vital, idiosyncratic force. (Could anyone really wish away the moment when she screeches, "I don't know nothin' 'bout birthin' babies!") No one is like her unless . . . it is Scarlett herself. Prissy is a comic grotesque, the dark mirror image of her devious, lying mistress. They are paired, just as the elegant Dilcey mirrors the style and competence of Ellen. Blacks and whites complement and complete each other in important ways, their intimacy a fact of life. Intricate and comical is the pecking order whereby the house slave Prissy can snub the madam Belle Watling. Perhaps it was the bonds of affinity and friendship more than the racism of slavery itself that bothered black intellectuals who saw and reviewed the movie. Melvin Tolson, a Harlem poet and critic recently featured (and played by Denzel Washington) in *The Great Debaters*, wrote that "*Gone with the Wind* is more dangerous than *Birth of a Nation*." Griffith's film "was such a barefaced lie that a moron could see through it. *Gone with the Wind* is such a subtle lie that it will be swallowed as the truth by millions of whites and blacks alike."

Recent scholars of black cinema like Donald Bogle and Thomas Cripps have taken a more nuanced view, acknowledging the racism but applauding the strength of the black presence at a time when there were few roles of color at all. (Scholars and critics have also begun to appreciate the glories achieved, within and despite a racist framework, by McDaniel contemporaries like Stepin Fetchit and Bill "Bojangles" Robinson, even in Uncle Remus.) Context is all, as is the realization, so foreign to literalists, that movies of whatever stripe or period inevitably distort history. In the arts, the activists of every minority and persuasion who cry stereotype have probably hurt more than helped their various causes (a more recent example being those who criticized the blaxploitation films of the seventies and virtually annihilated that charming and idiosyncratic subgenre of the action film). In the name of underdog solidarity, they practice elitism, afraid of what audiences will think if left to their own devices. If the servility of blacks in *Gone with the Wind* strikes some as offensive, it is closer to the reality of the period than Mammy's overweening strength and authority. Yes, house slaves were in a better position and could be snobs to boot, but Mammy goes way beyond that, becoming the mother of us all, an all-powerful, all-nurturing fantasy in which both blacks and whites, males and females, have taken comfort. For Mitchell's purposes, it is really Mammy whom Scarlett longs for. When she cries for Tara, it isn't so much the red clay that invites her home but the great black bosom, the metaphorical earth mother and resting place, of the little girl forced to grow up too soon.

Impermissible currents of interracial attraction, fear, and affinity appear in twisted and devious ways, hide but never disappear. As Leslie Fiedler has intimated, the image of the oversexualized black male is deflected, displaced onto Rhett—hence his affinity with Mammy. Hence also Mitchell's sudden need to distance herself from him by offering up drawing-room actors in preference to Clark Gable.

On the other side, Prissy as comic relief with Mammy as safe harbor represents the whole tradition of desexualizing the black female: nowhere do we find the young and pretty blacks and mulattoes whose enforced relations with their masters humiliated both slaves and mistresses, the concubines who presented the planters' children with half-brothers and -sisters.

Hattie McDaniel, a former song-and-dance performer and vaudevillian (Susan Myrick and Peggy Mitchell thought her too broad for the role), made her way to Hollywood and eventually became the best-known screen maid of all time. She succeeded in movies despite the color barrier, making more than a hundred films between 1931 and her death in 1952 and playing alongside Clark Gable, Jean Harlow, Henry Fonda, Shirley Temple, and Katharine Hepburn.

Though usually cast as a domestic, McDaniel occasionally got her licks in, throwing a drink at Henry Fonda in *The Mad Miss*

Manton (1938). One long, delicious act of sabotage came in 1936's *Alice Adams*, when she played the outrageously bossy maid to the social-climbing Adamses. A sort of anti-Mammy, she won't be inconvenienced by her employers' needs or put up with the airs of the affected Alice (Hepburn), who refers to her as "la domestique." The pièce de resistance comes when the rich boy Hepburn is trying to snare comes for dinner and McDaniel disgraces the family at the table. Her impudence was too much not only for the Adamses but for critics, who attacked her character as entirely too independent and impertinent.

Her triumph in *Gone with the Wind* was neither unequivocal nor unmixed. Bowing to pressure from the mayor of Atlanta, who feared racial incidents at the great event, Selznick canceled the appearances of McDaniel, Oscar Polk, and the other black performers at the Atlanta premiere. An equally shocking bit of whitewashing came with the programs issued at the film's opening: the main one showed pictures of the major performers, but a separate edition was printed for the still very segregated South, eliminating McDaniel's photograph. Later, a further humiliation: Hattie McDaniel was the first African American to win an Oscar, yet at the Academy Award banquet at the Coconut Grove, the white cast members of *Gone with the Wind* sat together, and at a separate table in the rear sat McDaniel, alone with a companion.

Then there was the black backlash. When McDaniel won her Academy Award, Mammys were stock figures, used to sell pancakes and household cleaners as well as serving the upper crust in movies, so the alarm activists expressed was to some extent understandable. Still, that reaction now seems unjust and cruel. After her immensely moving acceptance speech, in which McDaniel expressed hope that she might be a credit to her race, NAACP head Walter White launched an attack. White had been a self-appointed watchdog during the filming of *Gone with the Wind*, urging Selznick to hire a black adviser on the set, and now he singled out McDaniel for racial betrayal. This woman who had known both sides of the domestic profession fought back with the famous quip, "I would rather make seven hundred dollars a week playing a maid than seven dollars being one." Another time she called attention to the fact that the light-skinned White was only one-eighth black and not qualified to speak for the race. "What do you expect me to play?" she asked, "Rhett Butler's wife?"

Even at the time, there was division within the black community, with some calling the film "a weapon of terror against black America," a glorification of slavery, and an insult to black audiences, and there were demonstrations in various cities when the movie was released, while others crossed picket lines and praised McDaniel's warm and witty characterization. Selznick, unnerved by the flare-up, had visions of going down in history as a racist in the manner of D. W. Griffith, who never escaped the charges of racist propaganda over *Birth of a Nation*. But the controversy was simply the first round of debate that would lead to heightened awareness, the civil rights struggle, and the triumphs of the fifties and sixties and better acting roles for black Americans, a debate about race of which Barack Obama's presidential candidacy is a thrilling climactic round. As for McDaniel, she became a force in Hollywood's black community, a benefactor and instructor to new arrivals (one of whom was Lena Horne, whose contract stipulated that she play no maids) and a door-opener to African American actors and activists while managing to stay on good terms with the establishment.

Butterfly McQueen had a rougher time. Spikier or simply less compliant on the set, she fought Cukor over, among other things, the childbirth scene: she refused to take Scarlett's direct slap (it was faked), but in return, she would express the extreme agitation he wanted. A former dancer and utterly unlike the simpleton she played, she found her life both wrecked and transformed by the movie. Everywhere she went, she was identified with *Gone with the Wind:* in the eyes of the world, she would always be Prissy. Exasperated with the limited roles on offer, McQueen eventually gave up acting and went on to get a bachelor's degree in political science in 1975.

For the impact of these two women on the film, we have to look beyond the literal. How striking, how stylish they are, how they put their stamp on a film that would be a distinctly lesser work without them. Being willing to make a bit of a fool of oneself—play dumber, crazier, more limited—is one of the great weapons in the character actor's arsenal and can create an interesting sense of tension between two sides of the self. If Myrick and Mitchell thought Hattie McDaniel too broad, too much of a grandstander, they may have detected in her excess a hint of irony, a barely perceptible crevice between Mammy as humble servant and Mammy as blackface performer (which she actually had been). Similarly, Butterfly McQueen ("I sho' is [a liar]") is so conniving, so ready to say anything her interlocutors want to hear, that she comes out the other side, alert with the furtive savvy of the underdog survivor. Even the high comic drama of the childbirth scene, when Prissy leaves Scarlett in the lurch, has a cunning twist. As a black woman pointed out, Scarlett finds she can't just snap her fingers—the "old reliable darkie" isn't so reliable after all!

In important if idiosyncratic ways, McDaniel's Mammy and McQueen's Prissy support the theme implicit in the movie's matriarchy, the increasing power and importance of blacks and women that in itself embodies the themes of Reconstruction as a historical force, one of a tide of popular middle-class social reform movements, a spectrum of concerns widening to include equality of race and gender. The term "Southern womanhood" must finally expand to include those other minorities obscured by the high drama of plantation dialectics, the exclusive "club" of mammy and mistress: field hands, house servants, free women of color, not to mention free white women of the lower classes.

And the ammunition for these impulses came in curious and sometimes devious ways. It is often noted that some of the framers of the Constitution, the very leaders who gave primacy to freedom and equality, were themselves slaveholders. As historian Edmund Morgan has suggested, some of these leaders actually grasped the notion of freedom from having grown up alongside slaves and witnessed human bondage. They knew at the time that slavery was wrong and would eventually be ended, but (aside from their own personal interests) felt that the freeing couldn't come at that moment without tearing the fledgling nation apart.

The South, with little in the way of a middle or urban working class, was very different from the industrial North, where women worked outside the home, as teachers and domestics or in textile mills and garment shops. There, too, outspoken women like Margaret Fuller, Lucretia Mott, Elizabeth Cady Stanton, and the refugee Grimké sisters took up the cause of women's rights. The Grimkés, whose abolitionism had made them unwelcome in their home state of South Carolina, also ran afoul of those Northern abolitionists who didn't want to couple the two issues. But Angelina and Sarah Grimké pushed both causes, writing eloquently about the "enslavement" of women and holding up a prophetic vision of female independence. Back home, they were virtually excommunicated, set up alongside the notorious Fanny Kemble as cautionary tales to Southern ladies about the perils of class betrayal. The upper-class women of *Gone with the Wind* are prisoners in their gilded cages, their status the prize whose price is freedom, their idealization the cornerstone of the myth of patriarchy.

"Ellen O'Hara was thirty-two years old, and, according to the standards of her day, she was a middle-aged woman. . . ." *Gone with the Wind* goes on to describe her self-effacing grace, calm and constant work, all of which goes into the service of Gerald O'Hara, her husband. And that is a two-way system. The planter patriarch is sustained by women, but his exalted position bathes them in reflected glory. Likewise with slaves: the greater their number, the greater the power and prestige of the woman who presides over them, and they in turn are elevated in status by the breeding and prominence of their mistress. For white upper-class women, accepting their own idealization means a conspiracy of silence and denial where the brutality and philandering of their husbands, often with slaves, is concerned.

The logic of female dependence, the enforced sense of vulnerability, rests on the idealizing and, more important, protective services provided by men. But with the war there's a crack in the facade. The absence of husbands opens up a chasm. Plantation mistresses are suddenly left alone to supervise slaves who are often unruly and likely to rebel. Along with fear, there are opportunities to be useful. Women take their domestic skills public, sewing and distributing uniforms, though stopping short of what scholar LeeAnn Whites calls "a politics grounded in independence for women." When the other world shakes, the inner world shifts, too. It's no accident that many of these women, as we've seen in histories by Elizabeth Fox-Genovese and Drew Gilpin Faust, now begin to write diaries and journals. These most often record their daily lives and struggles, their sins of omission and commission, and their prayers to God for self-improvement. With the contract temporarily dissolved, we see the beginning of a discrete sense of self, apart from the system. These women were far from expecting to publish their writings—personal ambition and self-display were anathema—but they could write about the world around them. There are many eloquent entries, if not on the level of Mary Chesnut or Louisa McCord, the economist who was the anti-belle to Chesnut's lively socialite. Like most planter mistresses during the war, Chesnut (unlike the widowed McCord) found herself constitutionally unable to do "real" work; nursing the wounded was intolerable. Like Scarlett and unlike Melanie, she's too squeamish to deal with suppurating wounds, too inhibited by ladylike inhibitions, and possibly too invested in her own vulnerability. Nevertheless she sounds a radical note. "Brutal men with unlimited power are the same all over the world." But as C. Vann Woodward says in his introduction to her diary, Mary Chesnut's feminist heresy is "interwoven with the antislavery heresy, and neither is completely intelligible without reference to the other. In fact they do much to explain each other."

She hated injustice to slaves, but even more she despised what slavery did to the masters' wives, children, and families, as well as to the masters themselves. "We live surrounded by prostitutes" and their offspring, she wrote. The men were probably "no worse than men everywhere—but the lower the mistresses the more degraded they must be."

Chesnut equated the plight of women with that of slaves, somewhat speciously, given their deeply different class differences. Still, the metaphor was not inapt—for her or Margaret Mitchell: "There is no slave after all like a wife," she concluded in a passionate tirade, explaining why Southern women whimper and whine. . . . And finally, "What a blessed humbug domestic felicity is."

What irony that domestic felicity would become the new shrine, the very salvation of Southern manhood! Once slavery was removed as what Alexander Stevens had called the "cornerstone" of white planter society, the hallowed home took its place. From the degrading image of Jefferson Davis being dragged through the streets of Georgia wearing his wife's scarf on his head, Southern manhood had to rise again, and the solution was a shift of vision away from the public realm. As LeeAnn Whites shows in her richly documented study of Augusta, Georgia, *The Civil War as a Crisis in Gender*, restoration of the old order was out of the question in an impoverished and chaotic postwar society where order itself could not be maintained. So the relationship between white men and their household of dependents became not only the focus of a new identity but a retrospective justification for the war itself. Defense of home and family were now served up as cause and inspiration, the role once played by Secession and the preservation of slavery. Confederate memorial movements, orchestrated largely by women, soothed the warriors, and allowed the women to enter the public sphere—not for themselves, of course, but in a carefully scripted subordinate role. (In death, as not in life, all deaths were equal. In cemeteries and ceremonies, class differences were conveniently erased.)

The campaign to restore wounded pride is one that Scarlett scorns but Melanie embraces. Nobly patriotic and sacrificial during the war, she becomes the grande dame of the Confederate memorial movement in its aftermath, persuading her friends to honor all the Civil War dead, not just the Southern fallen. With a powerful motherliness disguised as sweet submission, she props up Ashley until the end of her life. Scarlett, on the other hand, never finds domesticity other than a bore. Flirtation was a tactic and a weapon, a means to an end, as she showed in the famous scene when, preparing to go into battle, she pinches her cheeks in front of the mirror at Twelve Oaks. With Ashley as her prey, she stands apart from herself, a masquerade of the feminine, as the mirror returns a gaze that is both her own and implicitly that of the man for whom the presentation is intended. Having learned long ago "how to conceal from men a sharp intelligence beneath a face as sweet and bland as a baby's," she is never more in possession of herself than when arranging herself for "surrender."

Scarlett is poised at one of those pivotal moments in the redefining of women's roles, a transition that is never a simple progression but is subject to periodic upheavals, when the entire catechism of traditional womanly virtues—piety, chastity, sacrifice, charity, living through and for others, and unflagging loyalty to family and country—virtues held up since time immemorial, seem to be turned on their head! In their place are offered such alarmingly worldly aspirations as self-fulfillment, sexual freedom, mobility, choice, and appetite for things and ideas beyond home and family.

In 1915, the very year Griffith's *Birth of a Nation* unleashed the specter of rampaging blacks, another movie struck fear of an equally malevolent force, the Female Vamp who saps the male of his élan vital. This was *A Fool There Was*, introducing Theda Bara (the erstwhile Theodosia Goodman of Cincinnati) as the "vamp," a sultry, dark-haired seductress who preys on the hero, John Schuyler, and by implication the Dutch-Anglo ruling class. Based on the Rudyard Kipling poem "The Vampire" and Porter Emerson Browne's play *A Fool There Was*, the film also incorporated eugenics-based "scientific" discoveries of the late nineteenth and early twentieth centuries. The vamp, here and in her various manifestations, is evil incarnate, proof positive of female sexuality as a degenerative disease and a handicap to evolutionary progress. In Griffith's sexual pantheon, city gals are overtly sensual, dissolute, and bad, rivals of (and eventual losers to) rural innocents, such as Lillian Gish in 1919's *True Heart Susie* (though Griffith's treatment of his doll-like actresses on the set was anything but fatherly). In F. W. Murnau's great *Sunrise* (1927), male lust and love is split neatly between the archetypes of City Girl (bad) and Country Girl (good). Some of the worst degenerates in *Birth of a Nation* are the characters of mixed blood. It was a time when

America was not just racist but especially xenophobic, hostile to immigrants, Catholics, Jews, and the emergence of women.

In this cosmology, it is cities—those melting pots, those dens of iniquity populated by women and foreigners and agitators of all kinds—that are the locus of the threat to American virility and vitality. Teddy Roosevelt championed physical fitness and the great outdoors as escapes from these murky and malign influences. The Boy Scouts would turn sissies into men.

The gentlest challenge in the new models of independent femininity came in the form of the Gibson girl, an outdoorsy madonna barely emerged from the Victorian age but uncorseted and unshackled, rosily athletic yet still modest in bloomers and middy blouses. She was succeeded by the more daring flapper, an androgyne in skimpy clothes. But however gleefully these two types might lend themselves to commodification in the new art of advertising and merchandising, their images projected a healthy autonomy. Unlike the sexual terrorist, the vamp, the Gibson girl and flapper seemed to be active women in self-styled roles, not fantasy icons designed by men.

But there are vamps and vamps. It turns out the real threat wasn't this heavy-lidded denizen of the night, swathed in black, signaling her evil intent from a mile away, but the perfectly healthy and high-spirited female whose looks were anything but sinister. Peggy Mitchell may have found James Cain's novels too sordid, but her own femme fatale could have given any of his a run for her money in breadth of harmful influence. And Scarlett's deceptiveness is her superior weapon. She looks like an angel, but isn't she in her own way the vamp who saps the juices of her suitors?

The dashing heroes of *Birth of a Nation* are the wimps and weaklings of *Gone with the Wind*. If ever there was a class that could claim defamation, it's the white male planters. What are her armies of admirers, whey-faced strutting toy soldiers, but victims of her blood-sucking charms? Could this be why the South lost the war? The Tarleton twins have a mother who whups them though she doesn't whup her horses. Baby-face Charles Hamilton woos (or is wooed by) Scarlett and, after one night with her, goes off to war to die of measles and pneumonia. Frank Kennedy, a little old maid, can't collect from his customers and is outwitted by his wife. Ashley Wilkes gives loserdom a high poetic sheen. Gerald O'Hara, a reckless drunk, falls apart with the death of his wife. By contrast, Scarlett is a generalissima on the battlefield of courtship and marriage. Sherman has nothing on the deadly belle-then-widow as she cuts a swathe through the rolls of Georgia's most eligible bachelors.

Even Rhett, for all his exceptional qualities, is no god to our restless heroine. Postwar Scarlett recognizes no obligation to burnish the male ego, a characteristic at odds with every ingrained instinct of the Southern belle. What Griffith embraces and Mitchell rejects is the need to restore confidence in the defeated male population. Griffith does so, of course, by placing the virgin sweetheart at the center of the melodrama, raising the image of besieged purity as banner and provocation. Southern womanhood, frightened and besieged by black (or black-face!) suitors, gives white men a war they can win.

But *Gone with the Wind* offers no such balm. Because Melanie was the kind of woman who inspired and consoled, because she was only too ready to reflect the male back to himself at twice his natural size, the most painful scene in the film of *Gone with the Wind* may well be the one when she sides with Scarlett against Ashley. In a desperate move to erase personal failure Ashley has decided to go north and work in a bank. Scarlett is horrified. Why in the world would he go north instead of staying to help her run the lumber business? "Because," says he, agony in his voice, "I'd bury any hope of standing alone." "Oh," she shrugs unconcernedly, "is that all?" The coup de grace comes when Melanie insists he stay—after all, Scarlett has done so much for them. Whatever one may think of Ashley—and surely that bookish sensibility is all too rare in the South and deserving of encouragement—there is tragedy in his all but complete emasculation by these terrifyingly capable women.

Earlier, when proposing to Scarlett, Rhett had expressed a wistful plea for the occasional harmless hypocrisy. "Sometimes I think you carry your truth-telling too far, my pet. Don't you think, even if it was a lie, that it would be appropriate for you to say, 'I love you, Rhett,' even if you didn't mean it?" She won't, but we half wish she would. The male ego needs a certain amount of flattery, and we need the male ego. If all Southern women had been ego-squashers like Scarlett instead of ego-strokers like Melanie, Southern manhood might have been knocked back on its heels, never to rise again.

For the effects of a Scarlett-type mass abdication of woman's duty, we have only to glance at the spate of slacker-buddy movies of the Judd Apatow genre, in which men are in full, raunchy flight from maturity. Surrounded by women both beautiful and competent, and no longer capable of playing helpless—Lysistratas who'll fornicate but won't flatter—the guys retreat into boozy, stoner fraternities. The need for male pride, even warrior pride, has seemed so fundamental to our way of being in the world—the impulse to look up to men one in which pleasure and necessity were inseparable—that its erosion has to be life altering. Scarlett's constant nightmare in which she's lost on a road, afraid and alone, is that of the motherless child whose beautiful dream—the romantic, someone-to-watch-over-me Ashley—is hollow at base. This is what marks Mitchell's irreverence toward patriarchy as heretical . . . and prescient. As the ideal of manliness has suffered mutation in an era that has come to find less use for warrior virtues than for other forms of expertise and that has seen the remarkably rapid ascendancy of women, Mitchell and her heroine seem to have paved the way for a social convulsion in which something has been gained, something lost. But since the taste for war never dies, seeks only a new excuse and a new vehicle to get the juices flowing and become fashionable again, there has been something deeply unsettling, yet eerily inevitable in watching as the new spokesperson for bellicosity and confrontation emerged: a *woman*. A Scarlett—who went by the name of Sarah Palin, vice presidential candidate—posing as a Melanie!

How can we help but have mixed feelings toward this beautiful bully of a heroine, for what is she after all but that most fearsome specter, that demon of male nightmares: woman as nature? Not nature in the sense of lustful, not as degenerative disease, but as amoral, with a will and instinct to survive at any cost.

An unevolved, unsocialized creature . . . in other words, an adolescent. In an early response to *Gone with the Wind*, Stephen Vincent Benet, whom Mitchell greatly admired, wrote praising the book and citing it as to an example of the stories you love when you're young, a perception that delighted her.

Inside the tinkling charms of a Southern-belle saga are the rumblings of a feminist manifesto. And the very thing that makes it easy to dismiss or overlook *Gone with the Wind* is what gave it legitimacy and vitality at an age when it counts. Because the challenge is posed by a girl whose credentials are anything but sterling, whose motives are almost entirely selfish, and whose age, sex, and philistinism make her an unreliable fount of wisdom, her critique is easy to discount. But for all the same reasons, it makes a deeper impression on young hearts than any number of exhortations from responsible adults.

Yet thanks to this voice, which in its strengths and limitations are the strengths and limitations of the book and movie, perhaps we shouldn't be too embarrassed to claim *Gone with the Wind* as our Young Adult masterpiece, the national epic of a Young Adult country, to stand humbly alongside (if not at the height of) the *Iliad*, the *Aeneid*, *War and Peace*, *Don Quixote*, *King Arthur and His Knights of the Round Table*. A central reason for its enduring appeal is the DNA it shares with such quintessentially American genres as film noir and screwball comedy. Appropriate to a young country (and industry) that has never quite managed to emerge from adolescence, where tradition is lamented for its absence and the sexes, less fixed in their places, jostle more overtly for power, the wellspring of the story is Scarlett and Rhett's battle for the sexual upper hand. *Gone with the Wind* endures, like the screwball comedy and film noir, because it has an edge, and the edge is that it can't make up its mind about sex and marriage and romance.

If Appomattox didn't settle anything, neither does *Gone with the Wind*, least of all its own place in the cinematic or literary pantheon. The Civil War is not resolved, the male-female power struggle is not resolved; on- and offscreen, the battle continues. Yes, finally and perhaps alas, *Gone with the Wind* does belong to us all.

Bibliography

Bynum, Victoria E. *Unruly Women: The Politics of Social and Sexual Control of the Old South*. Chapel Hill, NC: University of North Carolina Press, 1992.

Cash, W. J. *The Mind of the South*. New York: Alfred A. Knopf, 1941.

Chadwick, Bruce. *The Reel Civil War: Mythmaking in American Film*. New York: Alfred A. Knopf, 2001.

Chesnut, Mary Boykin. *Mary Chesnut's Civil War*. Edited by C. Vann Woodward. New Haven: Yale University Press, 1981.

Cobb, James C. *Away Down South: A History of Southern Identity*. New York: Oxford University Press, 2005.

Cronin, Jan. "The Story That Belongs to All of Us." *Literature Film Quarterly* on *LookSmart* 2007.

Davis, Bette. *The Lonely Life: An Autobiography*. London: Macdonald, 1963.

Ebert, Roger. "Gone with the Wind." *Chicago Sun Times*, June 21, 1998.

Edwards, Anne. *Road to Tara: The Life of Margaret Mitchell*. New York: Dell, 1983.

Eyman, Scott. *Lion of Hollywood: The Life and Legend of Louis B. Mayer*. New York: Simon and Schuster, 2005.

Faust, Drew Gilpin. *Mothers of Invention: Women of the Slaveholding South in the American Civil War*. Chapel Hill: University of North Carolina Press, 1996.

Fiedler, Leslie A. *What Was Literature? Class, Culture, and Mass Society*. New York: Simon and Schuster, 1982.

Fitzgerald, F. Scott. *The Beautiful and Damned.* New York: Charles Scribner's Sons, 1922.

———. *The Letters of F. Scott Fitzgerald.* Edited by Andrew Turnbull. New York: Charles Scribner's Sons, 1983.

———. *This Side of Paradise.* New York: Charles Scribner's Sons, 1920.

Foner, Eric. *Forever Free: The Story of Emancipation and Reconstruction.* New York: Alfred A. Knopf, 2006.

———. *Politics and Ideology in the Age of Civil War.* New York: Oxford University Press, 1980.

Fox-Genovese, Elizabeth. *Within the Plantation Household: Black and White Women of the Old South.* Chapel Hill: University of North Carolina Press, 1988.

Gone with the Wind. Directed by George Cukor, Victor Fleming, and Sam Wood, 1939. 4-DVD box set, "Collector's Edition." Burbank, CA: Warner Home Video, 2004.

Greene, Graham. *Reflections.* London: Reinhardt in association with Viking, 1990.

Hahn, Steven. "The Other American Revolution." *New Republic,* August 7, 2006.

Harris, Warren G. *Clark Gable: A Biography.* New York: Random House, 2002.

Haver, Ron. *David O. Selznick's Hollywood.* New York: Random House, 1987.

Huang, Carol. "Tomorrow Is Another Day." *American Scholar,* Autumn 2006.

James, William. "The Moral Equivalent of War." In *The Best American Essays of the Century.* Edited by Joyce Carol Oates and Robert Atwan. Boston: Houghton Mifflin, 2000.

Kazan, Elia. *Elia Kazan: A Life.* New York: Alfred A. Knopf, 1988.

Lambert, Gavin. *GWTW: The Making of Gone with the Wind.* Boston: Little, Brown, 1973.

Lively, Robert A. *Fiction Fights the Civil War: An Unfinished Chapter in the Literary History of the American People.* Reprint ed. New York: Greenwood, 1973.

McGill, Ralph. *The South and the Southerner.* Boston: Little, Brown, 1963.

McPherson, James M. *Abraham Lincoln and the Second American Revolution.* New York: Oxford University Press, 1990.

———. "The Great Betrayal." *New York Review of Books,* November 30, 2006.

McWhiney, Grady. *Cracker Culture: Celtic Ways in the Old South.* University: University of Alabama Press, 1988.

Mitchell, Margaret. *Gone with the Wind.* New York: Macmillan, 1936.

———. *Margaret Mitchell: Reporter.* Edited by Patrick Allen. Athens, GA: Hill Street, 2000.

———. *Margaret Mitchell's Gone with the Wind Letters, 1936–1949.* Edited by Richard Harwell. New York: Macmillan, 1976.

Morgan, Edmund S. *American Slavery, American Freedom: The Ordeal of Colonial Virginia*. Reprint ed. New York: W. W. Norton, 2003.

Myrick, Susan. *White Columns in Hollywood: Reports from the GWTW Sets*. Macon, GA: Mercer University Press, 1982.

Perkerson, Medora. *White Columns in Georgia*. New York: Rinehart, 1952.

Pyron, Darden Asbury. *Southern Daughter: The Life of Margaret Mitchell*. New York: Oxford University Press, 1991.

Sarris, Andrew. *The American Cinema: Directors and Directions, 1929–1968*. New York: Dutton 1968; reprint ed., New York: Da Capo, 1996.

Sauter, Michael. "Love Lives of Laurence Olivier and Vivien Leigh." Available at: http://www.dycks.com.

Selznick, David. *Memo from David O. Selznick*. Selected and edited by Rudy Behlmer. New York: Viking, 1972.

Sowell, Thomas. *Black Rednecks and White Liberals*. San Francisco: Encounter, 2005.

Tate, Allen. "Faulkner's 'Sanctuary' and the Southern Myth." *Virginia Quarterly Review*, Summer 1968.

Thomson, David. *Showman: The Life of David O. Selznick*. New York: Alfred A. Knopf, 1992.

Tocqueville, Alexis de. *Democracy in America*. Vol. 2. New York: Penguin Classics, 2003.

Tolson, Melvin. "Gone with the Wind." In *American Movie Critics: An Anthology from the Silents until Now*. Edited by Phillip Lopate. New York: Library of America, 2006.

Walker, Alexander. *Vivien Leigh: The Life of Vivien Leigh*. London: Weidenfeld and Nicolson, 1987.

Warren, Robert Penn. *New and Selected Essays*. New York: Random House, 1989.

Waterbury, Ruth. "A Love Worth Fighting For." *Photoplay*, December 1939, cited by Alexander Walker.

Whites, LeeAnn. *The Civil War as a Crisis in Gender: Augusta, Georgia, 1860–1890*. Athens: University of Georgia Press, 2000.

Wilson, Edmund. *Patriotic Gore: Studies in the Literature of the American Civil War*. New York: Farrar, Straus and Giroux, 1962.

Woodward, C. Vann. *Origins of the New South, 1877–1913*. Baton Rouge: Louisiana State University Press, 1971.

Young, Stark. *So Red the Rose*. New York: Charles Scribner's Sons, 1935.

Acknowledgments

I want to express my gratitude to the Yaddo Corporation for giving me that greatest of all gifts, a month of solitude as I embarked on the writing of this book. Thanks also to the New York Society Library, the Westhampton Free Library, the Quogue Library, and the resources of the Suffolk County Library System—in combination, these provided me with every book I needed.

I am indebted to Jonathan Brent at Yale University Press and Mark Crispin Miller, editor of the Icons of America series, for the idea of having me write a book on *Gone with the Wind*. For research, Bronwen Dickey, my "Hertog fellow," and Eric Monder were invaluable, as in many other ways were Jonathan's assistant, Sarah Miller, and my sharp-eyed manuscript editor, Laura Jones Dooley. Thanks also to Stephen Deutsch and Donna Shaw for responding to computer-related distress signals.

And for reading the manuscript and offering suggestions at crucial moments, I am deeply grateful to James Naremore, Alan Trachtenberg, Frances Kiernan, David Thomson, Brenda Wineapple, and my agents, Georges and Anne Borchardt.

Index